FROM QUANTU

A Physicist's Journey to Mind and Healing

JOHANNA BLOMQVIST

Translated by Tuula Yrjö-Koskinen

1

Mindstream Publishing

Helsinki, Finland, 2018

Copyright © Johanna Blomqvist 2018

ISBN 978-952-94-0418-6 (paperback)

ISBN 978-952-94-0419-3 (EPUB)

Cover photo: Felix Mittermeier, Pixabay

Johanna's photo: Mari Lahti

TABLE OF CONTENTS

FOREWORD

From Quantum Physics to Energy Healing is a book about energy healing. It deals with my experiences on the subject, and how I found answers through research, quantum physics, the mind and consciousness. The "energy" that we talk about in this context is not "traditional" physical energy. In short, energy healing includes many different methods that influence well-being on a deeper level than the visible world. Among the best-known energy healing methods are Reiki, Quantum Touch, Pranic Healing, Healing Touch and Therapeutic Touch. There are also many variations of the above.

I am particularly familiar with the Bengston Method and Reiki, both of which can be studied on a number of courses. The method that I use myself is a mixture of the two, combined with other techniques that I consider to be effective. In the book, I deal with the common concepts behind the different energy healing methods based on my own experience, without attempting to describe the various techniques more detailed. Energy healing is a very personal, subjective experience, and treatments differ from each other, just as treatment sessions also vary from one session to another. In healing, however, the focus is always on the personal experience of the subject being treated.

At the time of becoming acquainted with energy healing, I had a doctorate in physics, earned ten years earlier, and was working as a specialist in computational physics and chemistry, providing support for researchers. I had a sound understanding of how the world functions and of the physics behind everything. So, just as for many other people today, the idea of energy healing was a challenge that I, however, had to accept for the sake of the interesting studies that I had found. As a researcher, I believe that we ought to be able to approach any topic with an open mind and let observations and data tell the truth. I was surprised by my experiences. As a physicist, I naturally set out to look for answers to energy healing from science. I sought answers to questions such as: Does energy healing work and if so, how? What is the "energy" transmitted in energy healing? What can science say about energy healing, if anything? What research has been done on energy healing? The book is divided up according to these questions.

The book has been written as an aid to those of you who wish to broaden their horizons. Could it be that your current way of thinking is not the only right one? Could you try to break your boundaries? A different viewpoint such as the one offered by energy healing can provide a new perspective both on us ourselves and on our own resources. Human being is still one of the greatest mysteries for us. Answers may be found from unexpected directions. This book is also suitable as an aid to those who are already practicing energy healing, yet need help in telling others about it. It is important to find a common language to explain energy healing and findings about it to the uninitiated. The book is also meant for you who may be seeking or would like to seek support from complementary medicine.

At the beginning of the book, I tell about my own path through energy healing and my experiences of it. If, however, you are immediately interested in reading about the scientific and philosophical aspect of energy healing, you can start by reading chapters 10 to 12, and then read the book from the beginning.

I hope you will enjoy reading the book. It is simultaneously a story of the change that has taken place in my own life as a result of energy healing, and an account of my journey from quantum physics to energy healing. After almost 20 years spent in the world of business and research, the interest sparked by energy healing finally took me into full-time lecturing and training on the subject of well-being, and to becoming an independent researcher focusing on the mind, consciousness, healing and energy.

Helsinki, May 2018
Johanna Blomqvist

P.S. In the book, I recount my own experience of energy healing and how I interpret it based on the science that I know. The way I see it, conventional and complementary medicine are not in competition with each other and are not mutually exclusive, but can complement each other very well. Each one of us is different as an individual and needs different treatment. The most important thing is always that the subject receives the best and safest treatment. So if complementary treatments without any adverse side effects can help, why not try them? Many countries are already talking about integrative medicine in which conventional medicine and complementary treatments are combined.

ACKNOWLEDGEMENTS

First of all, I am thankful to all the people who have influenced my thinking and supported me during the different phases of my life, including my family and friends. The list of names is too long to include here; you know who you are. Each and every one of you has led me toward this book. At the subatomic level, we are all part of the same, vibrating energy.

I want to express a special thanks to a few people, without whom this book would not exist.

First, I wish to thank Professor William Bengston, who is a pioneer in the field of research on energy healing. The world needs those who have the courage to tell their own view, even if it differs from the views of the mainstream.

I also want to thank my Reiki teacher Sari McGlinn, who introduced me to the fascinating world of Reiki. You have been my spiritual mentor whom I can always turn to.

This book would also not exist without my healees and the people who have participated in my courses. I am grateful for having been able to share this journey of exploration with you! Often, we have been equally amazed by the experiences of energy healing, and totally astonished after a treatment! I would like to express my heartfelt thanks to the dog, Melli, and to Melli's owners. Melli is special, and she has taught us all. If only we knew what she has thought about it all behind her wise eyes.

Thank you to my sister-in-law Maria, who told about my energy healing treatments to Melli's owners and many others. Thank you also for your comments on the text! It is wonderful to receive support from someone so close who has chosen the same path.

Thank you to Dr. Harri Virolainen and Dr. Ilkka Virolainen for your valuable comments on my book. Thank you also to the publisher of my Finnish book Viisas Elämä, and especially to Batu and Kosti! As an author who was having her first book published, I received the help that I needed from you.

I highly value the comments of Samu Mielonen on the English text. Thank you!

Rajatiedon Yhteistyö ry. is gratefully acknowledged for financial support.

I am deeply thankful to my husband Anssi, for supporting me in this project, too. I don't just mean all the discussions, the issues we have thought about together, or the late hours. I also mean all the ideas about what could be studied, your ability to see connections, and, of course, the enthusiasm to get and to build the most various equipment to support the research. We really are one. <3

Finally, I would like to thank my children Teo and Stella, as well as my "colleague", the cat Otto. Thank you for your support and love! I hope to be able to pass on at least a part of all the goodness and the positivity that I receive from you.

I wish to dedicate this English translation of the book especially to Otto, who recently passed away. One era ended when you left us. Like your soul is now free to fly anywhere, I want to send this book to the world, to find its way to those who need this.

INTRODUCTION

This book is a story of my research journey into the world of energy healing. It tells how I got to know about energy healing, how I learned it and what kind of experiences I encountered in my treatments. As a physicist, I wanted to find answers to my questions from science and research. What can science say about energy healing? What research has been done on the subject and how can it be studied? I wanted to look into energy healing with no preconceptions, just as with any research problem, and to try to understand it better. In my doctoral thesis ten years earlier, I had done quantum mechanical calculations for molecules, modeling biodegradable plastics in order to obtain a molecular model on interactions that would be as precise as possible for the design of better materials.

The first time I got to know about energy healing, I was in my dream job and, in my opinion, had some kind of understanding of how the world works and the physics behind everything. I first heard about energy healing in summer 2011. I started to hear accounts from many sources about various diseases and disorders for which conventional medicine had no cures. These included arterial hypertension, Crohn's disease, thyroid disorders and cancer. The only choice, if any, was to take palliative medication until the end. I wanted to help, so I began to look for possible complementary methods of treatment. At least it would do no harm.

The first thing that I acquainted myself with in the world of complementary medicine was the energy healing method developed by Dr. William Bengston, along with his research. Bill Bengston has conducted decades of research on energy healing. After carrying out treatments and encountering many cases of healing, he ended up in a laboratory wanting to learn to better understand healing. Through laboratory tests, he studied, among other things, how mice recovered from fatal types of mammary cancer. The effectiveness of the method had been proven in several studies, which was exceptional, given that the method is complementary treatments. The Bengston Method is a hands-on healing method, which uses a technique that he has developed and works at the level of the mind. Treatment can also be carried out at a distance, treating subjects from thousands of miles away. Bill Bengston has also written a book about his research. His publications and the book describe his research - it could be any generally approved topic of research.

The idea of energy healing was a challenge for me. Could you really influence healing by channeling energy through the hands, with the possible assistance of the mind? Research, however, did not give me any reason to reject the Bengston Method, so I set out to study it, with the desire to learn more about energy healing. In Chapter 2 of this book, I tell more about research on Bengston's energy healing. I was also interested in Reiki, which seemed to be one of the basic methods: a method from which many other energy-healing methods have originated. Reiki also seemed an easy method to learn, unlike the Bengston Method.

Reiki is often presented as a Japanese method of natural treatment (in Japanese *Usui Shiki Reiki Ryoho*) and a form of energy healing. Originally, a method of inner growth, it is said to promote and maintain the well-being of the practitioner, and it can also be used to promote the healing of others, to relieve pain, to help with relaxation and to support well-being. As in the Bengston Method, the Reiki practitioner does hands-on healing, transmitting a "universal life force" into the subject through his or her hands. The universal life force is described as energy that flows constantly, both within and around us. Its existence can be felt in the body, mind, and life in general, and can be felt even if there is only a little of it. Reiki can also be sent to someone else as distance treatment, i.e., it can be used to treat someone who may be hundreds or even thousands of miles away. Reiki was a challenge to mind used to logical, rational thinking. If you are used to living in the Western materialistic world, it is difficult to accept the effect of the mind on healing. I was particularly surprised by the fact that in Reiki, it seemed that nothing was done, although I learned later that a lot was happening beneath the surface. A Reiki practitioner merely holds the hands above the subject being treated or touches them lightly. I decided, however, to give Reiki a chance. In Chapter 3, I tell more about the Reiki method and, in Chapter 4, how I learned energy healing. I considered it important to tell how I learned energy healing and what kind of energy healing, because energy healing can be done in various ways.

Reiki is taught on courses, and it became my hobby to attend Reiki courses and to treat my relatives, friends and an increasing number of people. I wanted to learn more about this strange healing energy and about what actually happened in treatment. I confess that I also created challenges in my own mind. You see, some people say that skepticism on the part of the practitioner may have an impact on the end result of the treatment. I had my doubts, and wondered whether energy healing could work at all. On courses, we discussed how it is difficult for a mind learned to use logic to reason to let go of power. If you are used to operating using logical, rational thinking, as you do in e.g., mathematics, it is difficult to change over to the intuitive side. The mind, that is the ego, tries to explain what is happening in the treatment and what isn't. It gradually began to dawn on me what Reiki and energy healing actually are, and what kind of work actually takes place behind the apparent lack of activity. The experiences of my subjects and the gradual accumulation of my own treatment experiences encouraged me to continue and to try to understand and explain what was actually happening in the treatment process. It also became gradually easier to recognize the general characteristics behind the different methods. I will tell more about these in Chapter 5.

Energy healing also seemed to contribute to my own development. Gradually, through different findings and sensory experiences, I began to learn more about healing. In Chapter 6, I tell about my own energy healing experiences and the experiences of my subjects. The case of a dog called Melli made a particular impression on me. Melli had a severe cancer tumor in her back leg but, during weeks of treatment, her tumor diminished in size, and she made a complete recovery. From the point of view of a researcher, a single case of healing is, of course, just an individual case, but Melli was my first cancer patient, and a dog at that. Since I also knew about Bengston's mice, almost hundred percent of which were cured, Melli's healing could not have been just a coincidence. I tell more about Melli's case in Chapter 7, and objectively about my own experiences in Chapter 8.

In addition to Melli's case, the stories that I was constantly hearing about the effect of energy healing gave me the incentive to find out more and to write this book. As a physicist, since the beginning of my learning about energy healing, it is as if I have existed in between two worlds, trying to find a connection between them. I will explain more about this in Chapter 9. In Chapter 10, I try to describe how the energy used in energy healing differs from energy normally dealt with in physics, and discuss whether this energy can be measured. I was especially interested in what science can say about energy healing, if anything? Chapter 11 concentrates on quantum physics and what can be said about energy healing based on quantum physics. It is often said that quantum physics provides evidence of the effect of mind over matter. Could it explain also energy healing? In addition to quantum physics, I was also unable to disregard the mind, the question of consciousness, the mystery of healing and the placebo effect. Can energy healing be viewed at all from the materialistic perspective from which we normally perceive the world? Energy healing gradually led me to some fundamental questions, to seek answers through the mind and consciousness, about which there is more in Chapter 12.

Anecdotes or narratives are individual cases, but when they form a bigger overall picture, they are no longer individual, but statistically more significant and something that research should also apply itself to. From an interest, therefore, in understanding my own experiences, I also began to seek out research information about energy healing. I also proceeded to carry out some initial research myself. You can read more of these in Chapter 13.

There are many questions around energy healing, at least some of which I hope to be able to answer in this book. There are millions of people in the world that practice Reiki, about 1 million of them are estimated to have completed the Reiki studies and reached the level of Reiki teacher, and the number is growing all the time. Simply because the number of energy healing practitioners is constantly increasing, we must learn to better understand what energy healing is and what it entails. Why do so many people gain - or think that they are gaining - benefit from it? It is also important to understand some subjective experiences such as how energy healing is experienced by the client and the practitioner. The last chapters are a compilation of some of my findings and insights gained during my research journey into energy healing – a journey that is still continuing.

ABOUT ENERGY HEALING

CHAPTER 1. Background of energy healing

The natural healing force within each one of us
is the greatest force in getting well.
- Hippocrates, 460-377 B.C.E.

Energy healing is an ancient form of treatment that has been practiced
for thousands of years.

If you study history, you will run into energy healing or hands-on healing in many contexts and cultures. To my surprise, I learned that energy healing was indeed ancient and part of a tradition encompassing almost all cultures. "Hands-on healing" is a form of treatment that originates already thousands of years ago. In the caves of the Pyrenees, discoveries have been made of 15 000-year-old cave paintings dating from the Neolithic Age that have been interpreted as depicting hands-on healing. References to hands-on healing have been found all over the globe throughout history. During centuries, for instance, the notion prevailed that royalty possessed healing powers and that their touch could heal even serious illnesses. The notion of the divine origins of royalty came from the Sumerians: they considered the king as an agent of God descended from heaven, and believed the supernatural powers to be a sign of a divine connection. Therefore, in Babylonia and Egypt, rulers were told to heal with the touch, and one will find descriptions of the laying of hands on the sick in Egyptian wall engravings and papyrus texts. It is also told that the Roman emperors, among them Hadrian and Vespasian, healed the sick through the laying on of hands.

Elsewhere in Europe, the "Royal Touch" or "King's Touch" was well-known into the 19th century, as several monarchs in different parts of Europe, including France and England, healed the sick through the laying on of hands. The ability to heal was believed to be hereditary and an indication of the divine origins of royalty. It was also told that scrofula, or lymph node tuberculosis, would be healed through the royal touch. When scrofula was raging, members of royalty would regularly hold big ceremonies, which were attended by thousands of people. Those who were healed would also receive a gold coin, thought of as an amulet, as a token for their visit. Seeking the royal touch was popular, and according to documents of the time, it was considered especially effective as a pain relief treatment and as a treatment of unattractive rashes, in addition to scrofula. Of course in the case of scrofula, you have to mention that it was rarely a life-threatening disease to begin with and that it would often heal of itself, too.

In old Christian texts, hands-on healing was considered as something comparable to prayer and receiving sacraments; after all, Jesus, too, did hands-on healing. In the Gospels of the New Testament, there are many references to the ability of Jesus to do hands-on healing. In the Gospel According to Luke 4:40, for instance, the following is mentioned:

> *At sunset, the people brought to Jesus all who had various kinds of sickness, and laying his hands on each one, he healed them.*

Jesus healed by laying his hands on people with leprosy and deadly fevers, as well as the blind and the deaf-mute, among others. It is also told that healing did not require faith from those who were treated. One can find similar stories in other religions as well, such as the Prophet Muhammad healing the sick and the blind. For instance, he healed a broken leg by merely stroking the broken part with his hand.

However, energy healing is most commonly associated with the spiritual teachings of the East. In the East, especially in China, India and Tibet, one can find many references to energy healing. The body's meridian system, the energy channels, through which *qi* or life energy flows in our body, originates from China, where it was developed thousands of years ago. When a person is healthy, energy flows freely to all parts of the body, whereas energy is weakened or blocked when a person is ill. Many Eastern forms of healing aim to influence the flow of the life energy. Formerly, it was common that the knowledge of healing would pass directly from a master teacher to his pupils. The Chinese book of medicine, *Nei Ching*, dating from about 200 B.C.E., is the world's oldest book on medicine and also the oldest tome that mentions hands-on healing. In the history of the Yin dynasty it is told (from the book Lao-Tzu, Tao te Ching: A New English Version):

> *Those who cultivate dao and nourish qi are able to channel qi to others.*

Hands-on healing is also known in Africa, South America and in the native American Indian cultures. Throughout time, people have been slightly afraid of these invisible natural forces. Shamans and other healers have received much respect and power due to their ability to "explain" or foretell upcoming changes.

Hands-on healing has raised many questions and each period has strived to understand and approach it according to the scientific viewpoint of the time. In ancient Greece, the father of medicine, Hippocrates, described in his writings dating from ca. 460 B.C.E. an odd sensation in the hands, as if a flow or "energy" would stream from the hands, affecting healing (from the book B.M.Dossey et al. Holistic Nursing – A Handbook for Practice):

> It has often appeared, while I have been soothing my patients, as it there were some strange property in my hands to pull and draw from the afflicted parts aches and diverse impurities.

Paracelsus, a German doctor and alchemist, described in the 16th century that hands-on healing was the outcome of magnetic energies. He believed that the human being held magnetic qualities, which attracted *mumia* or the life force. *Mumia* is an essential prerequisite for healing; when it decreases, life stops, and when it increases, life flourishes. Also, at the end of the 18th century, the German doctor Frank Mesmer studied how life energy, which seemed to have magnetic nature, affected healing. He referred to it as "animal magnetism", which was a kind of liquid that filled the universe. Mesmer's patients felt an unusual stream or flow in their bodies during the treatment, until they experienced a form of "healing crisis", which led to healing. At first, Mesmer used magnets as an aid, but then realized that he could achieve the same effect by setting his hands over the patient's body. A scientific commission of the time rejected Mesmer's studies as being "philosophically untenable". Both Mesmer and Paracelsus remain controversial figures in history. They have been thought of as forerunners, but also as charlatans.

With the discovery of electricity and magnetism, similarities between different energy forms also began to be perceived. At the end of the 18th century, the Italian physicist Luigi Galvani described how life energy, similar to electricity or magnetism, seemed to radiate from the Sun, and how it had the capacity to affect metal, water and wood. Life energy seemed to permeate everything; it flowed in and through the human being with the breath and streamed out from the fingertips. Galvani is best known for his frog studies, whereby he observed the electricity in the muscles, which he also referred to as animal electricity. In the 19th century, electricity and magnetism, and their effect on health, were increasingly studied. At the end of the 19th century, there were an estimated 10 000 therapists in the United States who used electricity for therapeutic purposes. Science and religion had separated already in the 17th century, and the mind and the body were commonly treated as separate, as Western science would increasingly focus on the individual functions of the different parts of the body. Also later on there have been efforts to study the possible electromagnetic flow from the hands. I will tell more about these more recent studies later on in this book. A good source of information on the most well known healers of our time is the "Yliluonnollisten ilmiöiden ensyklopedia" by Dr. Harri Virolainen ja Dr. Ilkka Virolainen, currently only available in Finnish.

Today, energy treatment, or energy healing, is practiced under many different names. One refers to Anomalous Healing, hands-on healing, paranormal healing, healing with intent, spiritual healing, laying on of hands, Quantum Healing, Reiki, Quantum Touch, Therapeutic Touch, Healing Touch, Pranic Healing, Distance Healing, qigong, or simply to Healing. There are so many terms that often the individual methods are hardly differentiated, either by the therapists themselves or by those who study the subject. Energy healers can also develop their own methods once having found a personally suitable way to practice energy healing. This is what William Bengston also did, and I will tell more of his method in the next chapter.

CHAPTER 2. Bengston's research on energy healing

"The day science begins to study non-physical phenomena,
it will make more progress in one decade
than in all the previous centuries of its existence.
If you want to find the secrets of the universe,
think in terms of energy, frequency, and vibration."
- Nicola Tesla (1856-1943)

In this chapter, I will tell about William Bengston's research and results,
which cannot be explained in the light of current science. Bengston's
studies were my first contact with energy healing.

In the summer of 2011, I began to pay more attention to the stories that I heard from several directions about various cases of people getting struck with serious illness. The only option that doctors offered to them was medication for the rest of their lives, although sometimes there was not even that possibility. In today's health care – or rather sickness care – the treatment is often the same: a pill and medical treatment that – perhaps - will normalize the situation. I attended a presentation by professor Arvid Carlsson regarding his research conducted over 70 years. Arvid Carlsson has participated in many studies and medication development projects: he has, among others, studied serotonin, adrenalin, dopamine and the precursor of Prozac. Carlsson received the Nobel Prize for medicine along with two other scholars in 2000 for his discoveries regarding the signal transduction in the nervous system. In the signal transduction, a molecule outside the cell activates a receptor on the surface or inside the cell, thereby affecting the cell's functions such as metabolism, gene expression or cell division. In his presentation, he described how a model had been created whereby many illnesses were treated with medication. Typically, medication is used to "block" the flow of information moving in the body, and to this end, gaining knowledge of dopamine and serotonin has been important. Actually, it is not treating, but rather obstructing the flow of information in the body that is taking place. The word "model" was a key term and an awakener for me as I had done years of work on my doctoral thesis, building various models in an effort to depict reality, which in my case had to do with biodegradable plastics. In my doctoral thesis, I began by experimenting with different ways to replicate a known, real situation, before the model could be used to create new kinds of plastics. The models worked in different ways depending on their purpose of use, some better than others. The word "model" thus struck me: if one also spoke of a model in the context of treatments, could there be other alternatives?

I became interested in the idea of another model for healing. Introducing foreign agents into the body and its immune system did not sound as the best alternative, as after all, a human being is not a machine. We still don't fully understand how the human body functions as a whole and what affects what. Medicine packages contain long lists of possible side effects. If the immune system is functioning properly, normally the body is able to cure itself. I wanted to better understand the workings of the human body, particularly its ability to cure itself, and thus began to search for more information.

You reap what you sow. My world view was first challenged in the summer of 2011 as I became acquainted with William Bengston's research. Doctor of Philosophy William Bengston works as a professor of Sociology in St. Joseph's College in New York. In the course of the past 40 years, Bill Bengston has witnessed recoveries from many illnesses, including difficult ones, such as bone, pancreatic, breast and brain cancer, rectal, lymphatic and stomach cancer, as well as leukemia. As his method, he has used a self-developed energy healing technique. The method included a series of routine mental tasks that were not directly linked to healing, and the mastering of which required several weeks of practice. The effect of the method developed by Bengston has been proven in several studies, at that time 10 experiments in total, conducted in five different universities.

Bill Bengston went on to study healing in more detail in laboratory circumstances in order to find an explanation for the healing cases that he had witnessed and to gain a better understanding of the phenomenon. In the first laboratory experiment, Bengston treated 5 mice that were injected with a highly lethal type of mammary cancer. The cancer was forecast to kill the mice with a 100% fatality within 14 to 27 days of the injection, and not one mouse ever made it beyond 27 days. Bengston treated the mice for one hour on each day during 30 days. At first, the mice's tumors developed a blackened area, which became more and more inflated, then ulcerated, burst, closed and finally dried up. After the tumor had disappeared, the mice lived a normal mouse's life span. Bengston also had a control group with mice that were sent to a different city just to be on the safe side. Two mice from the control group died within the forecast timeframe, and the remaining four were in poor condition at the time of the others' death. After the death of the two mice, Bengston visited the remaining mice in the control group. He could not get the mice out of his mind. Later on, Bengston suspected that this very fact might have affected the final result: all the four mice in the control group healed and lived beyond 27 days.

Never before had a single mouse infected with this particular type of mammarian cancer survived longer than 27 days after the injection. The results were so incredible that repeat experiments were conducted in different universities. This time, the healers were volunteers, the most skeptical of which where selected for the job, and to whom Bengston taught the method. In the new experiments, 91,7% of the mice treated with the method were healed. In the following chart, I have collected the results of five experiments conducted by Bengston (more detailed information on the articles can be found in the list of references).

Experiment	Number of mice	Number of healed mice	% of cured
Experiment 1			
Treated group	5	5	100 %
Control group on site	6	4	66,7 %
Experiment 2			
Treated group	7	7	100 %
Control group on site	6	4	66,7 %

Experiment	Number of mice	Number of healed mice	% of cured
Experiment 3			
Treated group	10	7	70 %
Control group on site	6	3	50 %
Control group off site	4	0	0 %
Experiment 4			
Treated group	11	10	90,9 %
Control group on site	8	7	87,5 %
Control group off site	4	0	0 %
Experiment 5			
Treated group	15	15	100 %
Control group on site	15	15	100 %
Total			
Treated group	48	44	91,7 %
Control group on site	41	33	80,5 %
Control group off site	8	0	0 %

The experiments also showed that there was a connection between the test and control groups: if anyone of the healers participating the

28

experiments visited the mice in the control group, some of these mice would also start to heal. The mice in the control group had to be taken out of the same building altogether, even to another city, in order to prevent a connection between the mice from happening. Bengston refers to this connection with the term *"resonant bonding"* and suggests that resonant bonding may also have a role to play in the placebo effect. With placebo one refers to the disposition to heal no matter what treatment is given, as long as those being treated consider the treatment effective. Resonant bonding may well be a more important factor than previously recognized. In many cases where the researchers, while examining the test and control groups, have noticed that the difference between the results of the two groups is too small, the reason could in fact be found in resonant bonding between the groups. When making such conclusions, the researchers succumb to type 2 errors, in other words they fail to dismiss a false null hypothesis.

It also turned out that those mice that had got rid of cancer would no longer get cancer, once they were re-injected with the same cancer type. This would denote that the mice had developed immunity to the cancer type in question, and that the development of a vaccine could also be possible.

I have to mention here that Bengston's experiments were not the first ones to treat animals with hands-on healing. Doctor Bernard Grad performed the first controlled energy healing experiments at McGill University in the 1960s. He studied the Hungarian healer Oskar Estebany's healing ability and noticed that Estebany could speed up by half the healing of inch-long wounds in mice in comparison to the control group. Estebany would treat the mice twice a day for 15 minutes at a time. Grad also studied the development of goiter by feeding the mice with iodine-free food. Estebany would again treat the mice twice a day for 15 months, and the thyroid gland of the treated mice grew considerably more slowly than those of the control group. Surprisingly, a similar effect was found when Estebany treated cotton wool that was then placed inside the mice's cages. That is to say that the healing effect was somehow charged into and conveyed through the cotton into the mice.

There is often talk, also in connection with energy healing, of the influence of faith, and of the placebo effect, on healing. When the person who is being treated believes that the treatment will help, the belief can create change for the better and lead to recovery. There has also been talk of the effect of the healer on the final result: either the healee believes in the effect of the treatment or at least the healer does. Bengston, however, claims that belief in the effect of the treatment is irrelevant. As a matter of fact, skepticism seems to be advantageous for the healer's work to be effective. Actually, Bengston cannot say anything about healing when the healer is a person who believes in the effect of the treatment. One could conclude from Bengston's research that faith in the effectiveness of the method is not necessary; rather, one can forget about the whole issue. There is no faith in the effectiveness of the treatment or any other ideology involved with the method, neither from the healees' nor from the healers' side.

Bengston has continued his studies and conducted, among others, research on remote healing, observing that neither distance nor time would seem to make any difference on the effectiveness of the treatment. He, too, has observed that cotton wool, as well as water store up "energy" produced by the treatment. Bengston has also studied the activity of the brain during energy healing sessions by means of EEG, measuring the electroencephalogram, and with fMRI magnetic resonance imaging devices. He has found some minor changes in the magnetic field in the vicinity of the subject. No significant changes occurred when the subject was close to the healer. In his most recent studies, he has noticed that the method would also seem to have an effect on Alzheimer's disease. There have also been surprises: to-date, Bengston has not succeeded in healing warts. For many energy healers, warts are one of the most quickly reacting ailments. Bill Bengston has written a book on his research and results entitled *"The Energy Cure"* – *Unraveling the Mystery of Hands-On Healing.* He is also Chairman of the Society for Scientific Exploration, which brings together scholars in the fields of physics, alternative forms of energy and energy healing, among others.

I was surprised to learn that Bengston's studies and their results had not been reported in the media. After all, we are talking about major research, in which cancer had been cured. Bengston's research results would seem to be too good to be true, and gained by means of a method, whose functioning mechanism was largely unknown. Energy healing is a method that is considered to be a complementary form of treatment, and healing, at least healing from cancer is not supposed to be possible. The method that has been studied is different from those that we are used to. However, you wouldn't think that the world could afford to bypass such results. An individual study that presents a different approach is easily bypassed, no matter how great the results, when, on the opposite side, there are thousands of studies following the existing way of thinking.

Bengston's studies awoke my interest. Here was a method that included instructions, so why should I not give it a try? A true scientist will not discard a method just because the topic is widely questioned or because it involves methods that contradict our current way of thinking. That's what research is all about: "to boldly go where no man has gone before", a line I can remember from the *Star Trek* TV series a long time ago. So I began to learn Bengston's method with the intention to try it out in my own treatments. In his article on the method, Bengston ponders whether you can even teach healing in the way that things are generally taught in schools and courses – should his hypothesis on resonant bonding be true. Instead it would suffice for the students to form a contact with the teacher, and this connection would influence all cases of healing. Thus, the actual healer would not be the healer who has learned the method, but the mere intention to heal and the established connection to the teacher would suffice to cause the healing. As a matter of fact, Bengston stated in his article dating from 2007 that as far as he knew, no one had learned the method simply from the written instructions. If I could learn the method from written instructions and use it to heal, this would suggest that resonance bonding is not so significant for healing, at least not in a single case. In this case, I will not have formed a connection with the teacher, unless such a connection can be born through the articles and the book, when studying the method.

An essential part of Bengston's method is work done in a routine manner, with no actual link to healing. No spiritual exercises or other spiritual activity are involved, like meditation or even relaxing. On the contrary: Bengston doesn't even recommend relaxing music or a peaceful environment for the healing sessions, but instead things to help raise the pulse, such as rock music. Bengston's method has its own technique, whereby the healer maintains a positive feeling, or an emotional awareness. Bengston calls it the "cycling" method, which involves rapid mental imaging. The method involves "cycling" through images of positive situations in one's mind, which helps maintain a strong, positive feeling, a positive emotional awareness, for a long time. As you cycle the images, you observe the feeling only from the outside, without trying to bring the actual situation behind the feeling back to mind. In contrast to other energy healing methods, in Bengston's method, the brain's activity is accelerated purposefully by cycling images in mind, instead of slowing it down through relaxation. It takes several weeks of training to master the method. At first one learns to cycle a couple dozen images per second in one's mind, and when this is mastered, the cycling is speeded up further using a cinema-like technique. When the technique is mastered, the actual healing occurs in the same way as in many other energy healing methods, in other words the healer lays their hands over the area to be treated or touches it lightly. Following their intuition, the healer treats as long as necessary, usually by scanning through the body and by searching for hotter areas that they will then give special attention to. During the whole healing session, they simultaneously continue the cycling in their mind.

Although Bengston's method does not include spiritual activity, it does have similarities with many spiritual healing traditions, where the shaman or other healer increases the power of the healing with their own techniques. These techniques serve to free the healer from their own ego and personal energy, and to create a "healing power" by observing their own emotions or physical sensations without getting attached to them. Bengston suggests that combining emotional awareness with rapid mental image cycling could actually create a kind of "magnetic-like flow" in the healing situation.

In Bengston's cycling method, the healer is required to make a personal wish list. It is important that the list is very personal: it has to include things that one really wishes for oneself. On the list, things are visualized as images as already accomplished. A similar kind of wish, or intention, is also used elsewhere; for instance in Sanskrit, it is referred to by the name *san culpa*, and used to manifest one's deepest wishes in reality. The method has similarities with the currently popular making of the "Vision board" or "Treasure map" where, on a board, you collect images and phrases of things that create a positive feeling and that you would like to experience personally. The board can be put up in a visible place to help gear yourself in that direction. As with Vision boards, when drawing up the list it is important to bring the situation to mind as vividly as possible, as if it was really happening.

So I began to think about a list for myself. Bengston offers clear directions on how to design the list. For instance, it is not worth listing that you want money, because in reality it is not money that you want, but something that money can bring to you. Therefore you have to choose an image of what you want to get with the money. The same applies, for instance, to health problems. When your knee is sore, you should not put a healthy knee on the list, but rather something that you can do when the knee is well. If, for instance, the list features playing tennis, it most probably means that the health problem has been sorted.

At first I could not think of anything. I really did not wish for material things. So I consciously sought for moments and situations that I would like to have more of in my life. Like a summer evening at the cottage, having a sauna and swimming in the lake, with the evening sunlight and the children laughing. After I got started, the items on the list began to come easily, and soon there were twenty things on it. Working on the list, and the learning involved were time-consuming processes, and I did not rush them. Every item on the list had to be dealt with separately in my mind, bringing back all the associated images and emotions, using all the senses. It was only then that the more challenging part would begin, the real learning of the method: the "cycling" of the images, trying to cycle the list in the mind as fast as possible. Already four images per second felt challenging. The underlying idea, however, started to emerge: the cycling will take the attention away from the treatment, or the goal, and instead, will focus it entirely on the feeling and on maintaining it. It was actually surprisingly easy to let the images that I was cycling guide me: it was as if an engine had started in my mind and begun to run on the screen. It was as if a film was run simultaneously in front of me and inside me. From time to time, as I was training, I could feel tingling in the middle of my head – a pleasant sensation. I wondered if this was somehow related to the pineal gland.

In spiritual contexts, the pineal gland is often associated with the opening of the third eye chakra, which in turn is linked to intuition and its development. At least this seemed to fit the current situation.

Giving an actual treatment with Bengston's method, cycling images in the mind at the same time, felt quite cumbersome, but I continued training the method regardless. At times, the cycling went well. For a few weeks, I took the habit of listening to educational recordings of Bengston's method as I was driving to work. In the recordings, Bengston drums the beat to mark the cycling speed, alternately slowing down and speeding up so that there is no way one can keep up. Sometimes, for instance when sitting at a meeting, I might suddenly realize that I had unwittingly started to cycle images in my mind: the images would start to cycle, first with the help of words, which I used to bring a certain image to mind, then as images. I would always hear Bengston drumming the beat in my mind, and sometimes I noticed how even my own finger would start to tap on the side of the table without me being aware of it. The cycling of the images would often be followed by a state of flow of some kind: it was easier for me to perceive the whole and the issue that we were dealing with as the ideas were bubbling forth. Actually the method felt like something that I could also apply to my own daily life to help make it easier.

Especially in the beginning, I experienced that it was easier to do the cycling while doing remote healing than while doing healing locally. When giving a remote healing session, it was easier to keep cycling the images while simultaneously holding the thought of the person I was treating. If my client was next to me, the easiest thing was to lay hands on their shoulders, listen and do healing, and cycle at the same time. If I had the feeling that I ought to move my hands away from the shoulders to another place, then I would do so, but it felt more challenging to scan the body for possible areas requiring healing. It was difficult to do the cycling at the same time.

I also began to think of other ways to get a similar effect and the same state of emotional awareness. In Bengston's method, images are cycled in the mind in order to maintain a positive feeling during the treatment and to keep the conscious mind out of the way. I was interested in finding out how healing was practiced in Oriental healing traditions. As it happens, they mention life energy, whose movements have been dealt with over thousands of years. Oriental teachings could help unravel something more about the "energy" of energy healing and provide a different perspective to healing. I became especially interested in Reiki, which seemed to be one of the basic methods and a method, from which many other energy healing methods had originated. Unlike the Bengston method, Reiki also seemed like an easy method to learn.

CHAPTER 3. What is Reiki?

Just for today

- *Be happy*
- *Expect the best*
- *Show compassion to all living beings*
- *Do your work diligently and honestly*
- *Be grateful for your blessings*

5 Reiki principles of life (gokai)

There are several different energy healing methods and the same method can be applied in many different ways. There is no single, unified view on Reiki either, and therefore I will describe my own interpretation of Reiki in this chapter.

Background of Reiki

Reiki, or the "Usui System of Natural Healing", *Usui Shiki Ryoho Reiki,* is a method of inner growth and well-being. The Reiki educational path was developed by the Japanese teacher Mikao Usui in the 1920s. Usui's goal was to offer a method to his students that would help them in their development. Mikao Usui collected traditions related to inner growth from various cultures, including Tibetan ones. Reiki, however, is not specifically related to any single culture or religion, and it doesn't involve a need to believe in any specific belief system. The story goes that Usui climbed to the top of Mount Kurama, in Japanese Kurama-yama, to fast for three weeks. While being there, he attained spiritual enlightenment and channeled a method of inner growth with its different stages, related attunement process, and healing symbols. Thus, Reiki wasn't initially developed as a method of healing, but rather as a method to help support inner growth. Reiki differs from other energy healing methods through its attunements or initiations, or reiju in Japanese. Attunements support spiritual growth, as each one of them is introduced at a specific phase of the development.

Reiki stems from the Japanese words *rei* and *ki*, which together refer to the universal life energy. Reiki teaches that there is life energy in every living being, human, animal and plant, and this is what discerns the living from the dead. Life energy moves within us and around us, and it flows independently of time and place. The flow of life energy can also be influenced, for instance with acupuncture needles. In addition, each one of us is surrounded with an energy field. The field of energy is dynamic; it moves and changes. An ailment, an illness or a particular emotional state can cause the energy field to change of to fall out of balance. The balance can be restored through the adding of life energy. The life energy helps create an environment conducive to healing. Our respective energy fields, or information fields, are also interconnected through a universal, all-encompassing energy field. Thus the healer and the healee are united through the energy field. In Reiki, the healer channels with their hands this universal life energy that is said to stem from the universe, or from the source, into the healee. The healer, in other words, does not give their own energy to the healee, but acts instead as a channel, in the same way as TV or radio broadcast programs. In Reiki, the healer places their hands lightly on or just above the healee, with the aim of facilitating the healee's own healing response. Thus, Reiki is a non-invasive form of treatment that does not penetrate the body tissues. The healers are taught to be open and to let go of the actual treatment so as to act as a mere channel to the universal energy. A Reiki treatment can also be given from a distance to a healee who is far away, or it can be used to treat the future or the past. In Reiki, healing takes place in a state where neither distance nor even time makes any difference. Everything happens here and now.

There is no uniform, widely accepted scientific view of Reiki and the mechanism behind it. Reiki is a method that is said to support the body's innate or natural healing abilities. Its effect is said to occur on a mental level, helping to quiet down and attain an inner, spiritual balance. Reiki healing is used to either prevent or to correct mental or physical states of imbalance. In the US, Reiki is considered as a part of energy medicine, and more specifically as a form of biofield energy therapy that deals with the body's biofields. A biofield could be described as a living being's information field, which interacts constantly with surrounding fields.

A typical Reiki treatment

In a Reiki treatment, the healer transmits or channels universal life energy into the healee. It is said that energy holds all the information that the body needs in order to heal. Sometimes there is also talk about transmitting specific Reiki energy, which refers to life energy transmitted by a qualified Reiki healer who has received all the Reiki teachings and attunements, as opposed to the transmission of life energy practiced by just anybody.

A Reiki treatment is usually conducted with the client lying down, clothes on, on a healing table. A Reiki session can also be given to a client in a sitting or standing position. In a Reiki treatment, the healer touches the body lightly or holds the hands a few inches above the healee's body. They keep the hands over each area to be treated for a few minutes, following their own sensations. The healer and the healee may feel the energy in different ways, most commonly as heat, sometimes as coldness, shivering, shaking, flow or pulse. Neither will necessarily feel anything in particular. Mostly, the treatment feels good and very relaxing. The healer's own sensations will often develop over the course of treatments, and the experience of energy flow will grow. Also, the intuition about the specific treatment required grows stronger: the healer feels how much and what kind of treatment the healee needs, and in which area. The treatment usually starts from the head area and proceeds toward the toes, but one can also start from the feet. In Reiki, one doesn't scan the body to find areas to be treated like in some other energy healing methods, but following their sensations, the healer can give specific treatment to areas that seem to need it. Most commonly, a whole body treatment includes 15-30 hand placements, sometimes also called hand positions. A whole body healing session usually lasts about one hour. Reiki can also be practiced as remote healing without the healee and the healer occupying the same space. A remote healing session usually takes less time than a local treatment, often about half an hour. Reiki is mostly used to help relax and to alleviate stress symptoms, anxiety and pain, as well as to support healing. A Reiki healer can also give him- or herself a Reiki self-treatment.

How to learn Reiki

Learning Reiki does not require previous studies. As a matter of fact, we all have access to Reiki energy, but there can be many causes that obstruct the connection. During the Reiki courses, the connection is opened and the use of Reiki is taught. Reiki healers are instructed to open up, and to be open to the flow of universal energy so that during the treatment they can transmit and channel this energy to their healees. In the training, you learn to observe your own thought patterns, and inner reflection.

For a long time, Reiki was taught as an oral skill from teacher to pupil, without textbooks or other materials. In other words, the manner of teaching used to depend, and still depends on the teacher: there is no established single standard of teaching or practicing. This makes the research on Reiki and the making of conclusions about the method more difficult. However, there are many things that apply uniformly for the entire field of Reiki. Usually, Reiki studies involve three levels, and once the healer has completed these, they will become a Reiki teacher or Reiki Master. Each Reiki level includes attunements that help open and strengthen the flow of Reiki energy. The Reiki attunements also strengthen the connection to the origin of universal life energy, and help to ensure that in the treatment, the healer transmits Reiki energy to the healee, rather than their own life energy.

In the original Reiki, *Usui Shiki Ryoho Reiki,* the fundamentals of the Reiki method are usually learned in a Reiki 101 course, Reiki 1, taught by a Reiki teacher, that is a Reiki Master. The course focuses mostly on self-healing, but it also introduces the subject of giving treatments to others. In Reiki, there is an emphasis on the inner growth and well-being of the healer themselves as a prerequisite for being able to treat others. In the advanced Reiki course, Reiki 2, one continues to learn more about Reiki and how to use it. The course focuses especially on emotions and on remote healing, as well as on developing local healing skills. There is also a continued focus on the healer's own well-being, spiritual growth and development. One learns to become a qualified Reiki teacher through the Reiki heart awareness course, Reiki 3A, and a teacher training period lasting several months, Reiki 3B. Each course, along with its related Reiki attunements, corresponds to a certain phase in the growth process. It is recommended that a few months break be taken in between courses, so that the student has internalized sufficiently the teachings of each course and is able to gain the most benefit from the next one. The Reiki courses provide a foundation for the practice of Reiki, but it isn't until you actually give Reiki healing that you truly start learning. After the courses, the Reiki path will just begin. Every treatment will teach more.

CHAPTER 4. My path to becoming an energy healer

Ego is just like a dust in the eye.
Without clearing the dust you can't see anything clearly.
So clear the ego and see the world.
- Unknown

Energy healing is not a simple, straightforward issue. Subjective experiences, and dealing with them, are an essential part of the process. In this chapter, I will describe some of the things that I faced at the time of learning the practice.

The journey begins: Reiki training course

Bengston's research results were the reason for me to attend a Reiki course. However, I was skeptical, and thought that I would attend a course only to see what Reiki is about. In spite of my suspicions, I was open and interested. The contrast was enormous when I stepped in from the sleety, grey November weather into the course space. I felt as if I was entering a different world. The space was full of stones of different shapes and colors, and filled with the warm light of salt lamps.

Now, years later, having taught several energy healing courses myself, I have met students coming to courses from various different reasons. Many have arrived on a friend's recommendation or inspiration. There are those who search for support to cope, those who want to help their loved ones, or to start giving treatments professionally. Someone may have come out of pure curiosity and will announce at the outset that they "don't believe in this at all". However, almost without exception, everyone has the desire to discover something within themselves: an inner resource to help support their own well-being and the well-being of loved ones. The first thing that a Reiki course focuses on is self-healing. This involves bringing the attention to one's own inner world and worldview, often to things that one has not even thought of or questioned.

Years ago, as I was attending my own very first Reiki course, I enjoyed the sense of ease and effortlessness, as well as the natural, positive atmosphere. For someone used to efficiency, order and logic, the course felt awkward: computers, PowerPoint presentations and minute schedules were missing. The course unfolded through discussions and by listening to the participants. Contrary to what people partaking in a Reiki course generally expect, I actually considered the discussions during the course to be more important than the Reiki initiations.

Mikao Usui meant the Reiki initiations and the Reiki path as a help to inner growth. It is said that Reiki initiations will contribute to the ability to receive and transmit Reiki with increasing intensity. Their purpose is to awaken and strengthen the healing power and natural flow of the life energy present in all of us. The initiations are always given at a certain point in the Reiki path. The purpose of the Reiki initiations is to open and strengthen the healer's connection to the source of Reiki energy. Opening and strengthening the connection will ensure that in a healing session, the healer doesn't resort to giving his or her own energy to the healee, thereby loosing his or her own health and well-being. Reiki is about inner work, and it is not possible to rush the internalization process.

The actual Reiki initiation is an experience that everyone will experience in an individual way. I experienced my own first Reiki initiation as a relaxing, peaceful and pleasurable moment. We sat next to each other on our chairs with eyes closed and hands in our laps, while the teacher moved around us. I listened to my own sensations and to what was happening around. Some colors, more than usual, passed behind my closed eyelids, as well as some flickering light and a pleasurable sense of relaxation. At times I felt warmth – nothing unusual. When I opened my eyes after the activation, I was surprised: all the colors around seemed suddenly brighter than before. I felt hungry and very thirsty. The person sitting next to me said the same. According to the teacher, this was normal and common: just like in the Reiki treatments, the Reiki initiation sets the metabolism in motion.

Later on, I have witnessed some very strong initiation experiences; the activation has brought emotions to the surface and made tears flow. Some people have felt pain in their back, heart or stomach area. Often the sensations are explained with the chakras. Chakras represent a concept derived from the Indian culture, of the centers of the human energy body. There are a total of seven major chakras. The chakra centers reflect the body's physical, mental and spiritual well-being. For instance, a feeling of pain in the heart area may be linked to the opening of the heart chakra; a similar sensation in the stomach area can be linked to life changes.

Reiki symbols are another essential part of Reiki for Reiki healers. The symbols work in different ways: they help, for instance, to form the

Reiki connection. The symbols teach the body how to get the treatment started and they act as tools that serve to teach the body a new skill. The symbols direct the attention away from the actual healing, away from acting through the ego and the conscious mind. Especially when learning to do healing, the importance of internalizing is stressed: internalizing and visualizing a symbol in one's mind before starting to use it. The Reiki symbols are said to be portals into Reiki awareness and the use of Reiki energy. Now, after some time and being more familiar with hypnosis and the functioning of the mind, I can see that the symbols are like the anchors often used in hypnosis. A hypnosis practitioner can create an anchor, which the person being hypnotized can use to bring back to mind a pleasant situation or feeling experienced in a state of hypnosis. Likewise, the Reiki symbols are used to anchor one's mind to act in a certain way.

In other words, receiving a Reiki symbol means inner work, as one forms a relationship to the symbol. The symbol is visualized, and it can be imagined as colorful, three-dimensional, vibrating and moving. The aim is to internalize what the symbol sets in motion inside and what it does to oneself and the healee. The closer the connection to the symbol, the less one needs to think about it, draw, or visualize it during the healing session; it can be enough to simply mention the symbol in one's mind. Symbols can be used at the beginning of the treatment: one can draw the symbols on both hands with your finger and repeat the name of a symbol in one's mind, and imagine how it is left vibrating in the air, opening up a healing space. Symbols can also be used in the beginning or in the midst of a treatment as a mantra. They can be recited silently in one's mind or even out loud, when needed, drawn in one's mind or in the air onto a desired object, such as a particularly painful area, to support the treatment.

In Usui Shiki Ryoho Reiki, one usually learns a total of four symbols. Each of the symbols has a different effect. *Chokurei* is for treating physical body. It is the so-called power symbol. The Chokurei symbol is the first symbol taught in Reiki, which, depending on the teacher is often given on the very first course. The second symbol to be learned on the Reiki path is the *Sei Hei Ki* –symbol, which heals emotions and thoughts. The Sei Hei Ki is usually introduced on the Reiki 2 course, like the *Hon Sha Ze Sho Nen*, which is the Reiki symbol for remote healing. *Daikomio* is the Reiki symbol for loving and heart awareness, which is received at the beginning of the Reiki master studies. Different teachers and Reiki approaches may give these symbols in slightly different stages of the Reiki path. In addition to these, other symbols can also be received.

Chokurei, the Reiki symbol for physical treatment, helps open the channel for energy healing. Chokurei trains the channel just like one would train a muscle. It teaches how to get an energy treatment started and how to strengthen its intensity. Chokurei helps create the right mindset. Visualizing the Chokurei symbol helps to attract a feeling and state conducive to healing. When one has visualized the symbol sufficiently and used it to create a connection to the treatment, it may be enough to simply pronounce the name of the symbol in one's mind, and a certain process will start. As I was learning the symbols, I imagined in my mind how the "Chokurei –ball" was revolving and as if throwing energy where it was needed. Chokurei penetrated deeply by revolving, vibrating and glowing like a golden, spiral shaped ball.

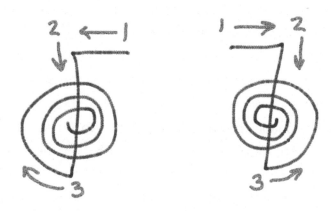

Fig. Chokurei symbol. Chokurei can be drawn either way.

To my surprise, learning to do energy healing did not involve any particular "energy work", by which one would aim to increase the flow of energy in the body and the hands. Reiki includes the idea that universal life energy flows into the body, often through the crown chakra, and from there on, through the heart, to the hands and feet. However, in Reiki, one only acts as a channel for the energy, without attempting to change the flow.

Self-healing is an important part of internalizing Reiki. According to Mikao Usui, in order to be able to help others, you need first to internalize Reiki sufficiently and to remove the possible mental obstacles to healing. In Reiki, there are no strict rules as to when you are ready to heal others. Each person will know it by themselves. There are also no strict rules regarding the treatment process, the hand positions during treatment or the length of the treatment. Instead, intuition plays an important role. Often the treatment is started from the head area, as this leads naturally to quieting and calming down, and to turning inwards. After the head, you treat the neck, the chest, and the stomach area, then the knees and ankles as well as the soles of the feet, unless there is a specific need to treat a particular area. Then you treat the back from bottom upward. It is possible to do self-healing sitting in a chair or lying down, just as when you treat another person. You can also treat just the chakras. According to my own experience from the very first self-healing session onward, a Reiki treatment calms down, quiets the mind and helps to relax. In the beginning, the sample hand positions, listed in Annex 1, helped me learn the self-healing. Hands are kept in each position for as long as it feels like there is a need to treat the particular area, often for a few minutes. The whole body treatment lasts about one hour. Instructions with images that can be used to learn the treatment positions can be found also in Foundations of Reiki Ryoho, pp.190-205 and in S. McGlinn's book Reikin luonnollisen parantamisen menetelmä (currently only available in Finnish).

Nowadays, when I teach Reiki in my energy healing courses, I recommend to start the treatment by drawing a Chokurei symbol on both hands and by creating a personal treatment routine. For instance, you can recite your own mantra or healing phrase to begin healing. Then you start the treatment by setting the hands on the area needing treatment. The hands can either touch lightly the area being treated or they can be held in the air at a slight distance from the body. Each person's own intuition will tell where to treat, and for how long. This applies to both self-healing and to healing others. The self-healing hand positions are helpful, you can also follow them when giving a treatment to another person: often you start from the head area, and then you proceed downward to the feet on the front side of the body, and then back up toward the head on the back side. It is also perfectly possible to start from the feet and treat toward the head, and then back toward the feet on the backside. There are no strict rules which you should follow.

When attending my first Reiki course, my mind was strangely quiet after the first day, as if I had slept and it was hard to wake up. The feeling was slightly unreal and I wasn't sure what to think. In the evening, back home, I gave a treatment to my husband, and he felt a clear difference to my previous treatments. Before the course, I had given him energy healing following Bengston's method. Now, there was more of a feeling of heat, as if the treated area had been warmed up, only the heat came from within, with a light prickling sensation. I felt the difference mostly in my own attitude: now the attention was on accepting the healing. I was aware of what I was doing; I let go, and listened to what was happening. I was simply present during the treatment, as if I was meditating.

The first time I received a Reiki treatment in a course, it left a lasting impression on my mind. I lay on the treatment table with my head on a pillow. Four course participants treated me; one treated the head, another treated the feet and two others treated my ribs, my stomach and my hands on each side. While being treated, I sank very deep. I heard all the sounds, but felt as if I was on a cloud, weightless. It felt hard to speak or to answer questions. I could have stayed there for any length of time; it felt as if time had stopped and lost its importance entirely. At that time, I was suffering from pollen allergy, and the student treating my eyes said that my eyes were glowing, burning hot. I could feel the warmness of her hands very strongly as she was treating me. Likewise, I felt heat over my left knee, which another of my healers mentioned. The meniscus of my knee in question had been torn and it had been operated half a year earlier. The knee was not fine yet and at times, it was in pain. After the treatment, I could no longer feel pain, and the knee felt as good as the other one. I have not had the pollen allergy, either since that treatment. When the treatment was over, it took me some time to come back to this time and place.

During the course, I started noticing differences as I treated various people. Almost always, there was a sensation of heat, but the heat was different compared to just holding hands over a warm area. I could feel the heat more in some places than in others, and sometimes it felt prickly, and at others, wavy. Some healees felt more open to receive healing than others. Sometimes I felt that I needed to treat specific areas more. Analyzing or scanning the healee's body in search for spots that might possibly require treatment does not really belong to Reiki. In the course, we treated the teacher's back, as it is difficult to reach your own back in self-healing. Her back seemed to absorb everything that would flow from our hands. Also, we all felt a cold shiver in the middle of the treatment, as if the wind had blown in between us, and simultaneously, there was a light smell of flowers. One of us brought this up, and our teacher said that she had just invited her own spiritual guides, or guardian angels, to assist in the treatment. It felt as if this may well have been the case...

What is energy healing? Did the Reiki course give me an answer to that question? The answers to these questions, after the first Reiki course were that "I don't have a clue" and "yes and no". In the course, I learned the basics of Reiki, how the treatment is given, as well as what Reiki is said to be and what it is founded on. My conscious, doubting mind did not get answers yet, only more questions and doubts. My subconscious mind, on the other hand, would say that Reiki was about love, pure love, total allowance and acceptance of both oneself and others, and that it didn't need to be explained, just experienced. It was a method, with which you could get a grip of your own spiritual development and of who you actually were. I was also left thinking, what was true. Is there even such a thing as a contradiction between energy healing and science? Could it not be that energy healing simply works? Does science state that it can't? In any case, I found myself thinking about these issues from an entirely new perspective. Instead of energy healing, my attention was now on my own attitude, presence, living in the moment, gratitude, letting go, and acceptance. Energy healing actually seemed to be more than just a technique. In order to help my conscious mind, I wanted to find out more about the real nature of Reiki.

Becoming introduced to Reiki felt as if a phone that I had lost a long time ago, had been returned to me. I felt strongly having now access to

53

a skill that I had once mastered, and then lost. With my newly found phone, I could speak with my inner self. As I left the Reiki course, I felt that my attitude had changed. I felt acceptance and was keen to find out what would ensue from this, even though my conscious mind was tapping on the shoulder and commenting that this could not work. I had no way of knowing what would happen next, but maybe for the first time ever that didn't matter. In a strange way, I was quite satisfied.

Self-debates

The weeks following the Reiki course were an interesting time, as I did self-healing and treated my spouse, our children, relatives and friends. I was quite skeptical, and I always had an expectation of what would happen or how the healee would experience the treatment. I also anticipated my own sensations - a feeling in my hands or a hunch where to treat - but in the early stages of giving treatments, I didn't feel much of anything, only a slight sense of heat in my hands. I was waiting to feel something that would encourage me to continue. My clients, on the other hand, felt all the more, and reported about astonishing sensations. For instance, I was treating my friend's shoulder that was sore from too much sitting at the computer, and as I held my hands slightly in the air above the shoulder, she described a strong sense of pain on the edge of her shoulder blade. I was just about to ask if she would like us to stop when she described having felt a sharp shooting pain, and afterwards, the whole shoulder pain seemed to have vanished. I was amazed, as I could not feel anything particular in my hands. I was even more surprised the next day, when my friend asked me what I had done in the treatment. The pain was still gone and the hand felt good, but in the evening, she had not been able to drink her favorite red wine. Others thought that it tasted good, but to her, it tasted awful.

So I continued giving treatments and noticed how I, too, would relax during them. Giving healing gradually started to become a way of life for me. I also began to let go of the need to feel something in particular during the treatments.

Currently, when I teach energy healing, I can see how something begins to arise in the mind of the course participants and starts to grow. With some, what arises happens on an emotional level. With others, the conscious, logical, analytical mind questions and requires more proof. One's own beliefs and worldview are newly weighed. During the course, I try to provide keys to how and where to look for answers. I recommend gathering data of personal treatment experiences and then making conclusions based on them. A course in energy healing is but a starting point on the journey within, to your inner self and beliefs. After my first Reiki course, I also belonged to the group that wanted to find more proof.

As a method, Reiki is simple and easy: after receiving the Reiki initiations in the course, one does hands-on healing. There are no specific, official rules as to how to treat. This is what can be seen on the surface, but the actual work happens elsewhere. After taking a Reiki course, the real work only begins. You have to work with your own ego or the conscious, logical mind. You need to find out, how your own ego reacts to the issue: does it accept that Reiki healing is so easy? For ego it is natural to think more critically, to reason, look for justifications and backgrounds. Ego questions things. It is obvious that the ego rebels and brings up issues; its task is to retain its own power and to prevent change. Reiki questions the ego's authority: your ego is no longer the sole ruler. The conscious mind has the tendency to seek cause-and-effect relationships, to draw conclusions and justify things based on reason and logic. By doing Reiki, the conscious mind quiets down in the same way as, for instance, in meditation. The conscious mind is bypassed and the unconscious mind, the subconscious takes over with its intuition, instincts and sensations. You gain access to your own inner resources in a new way.

Almost every Reiki healer needs to faces their own ego at some point in their Reiki path, sometimes more than once. We have grown up living in a world where reason and logical thinking are taught, to guide us and to take us forward in life. At school, we mostly learn to use our reason, and the unconscious, subconscious mind, that is the part that holds our imagination, is not given so much attention, or at least it is not actively practiced. Often, especially with the mathematically gifted and those who constantly use their logical thinking, it takes more time to learn now to act in a different way. When we start working more with the area of the unconscious mind, the conscious mind or ego resists. This is only natural, as for years one has acted differently. Both the unconscious and the conscious mind are needed, and at best, they work well together.

For me, at first each healing session was a clash with my ego and my own way of thinking. Reiki offered a tool for dealing with these kinds of situations, too. While doing self-healing, my attention was on the performance, and yet, I would suddenly notice that I seemed to float without thoughts. I would simply do self-healing and listen to the feeling in the hands and in the place being treated. I paid attention to the thoughts that were set off by the treatment. I even felt excitement as I anticipated the thoughts that would surface, as they seemed so strange and surprising. It felt like they were somehow associated with the treatment that I was giving; that I was reacting to it. The thoughts and feelings that the treatment would bring up felt like a sign, showing me what I needed to treat. If something felt disturbing, it needed to be faced and worked through, and then released. Each treatment felt different, bringing up different issues.

At first, I attempted to give myself Reiki self-healing on a daily basis. Mostly, I would try to cover the whole series following the hand positions of Annex 1. Often, I would treat at least the area of the head. I might treat my knees and stomach on the bus or on the subway. Before entering a meeting, I would treat the area of the head and especially the forehead, the neck and the area of the heart. I followed my intuition and treated those areas that seemed to need healing, and for as long as that feeling lasted. If I was tense, I treated the heart and the area of the stomach, in other words the places where I could feel the tension and that my intuition told me to treat. Increasingly, I started noticing a clear connection between my bodily reactions and frame of mind. It was also interesting to notice that my experiences fit together with the research that had been conducted on the topic. The results obtained by a group of Aalto University's brain researchers, led by Lauri Nummenmaa, indicate where emotions are felt in the body. They studied the changes that the persons participating the experiment felt in their body as they experienced different emotions, induced with words, stories and images. Over 700 people took part in the experiment from Finland, Sweden and Taiwan. In the study, a bodily map of emotions was created, showing how people experienced the emotional states in their body. In the study, it was found that positive feelings created the strongest bodily sensations. Especially the feelings of love and happiness led to strong sensations in the area of the head and stomach. Also, similar results have been obtained in the American HeartMath Institute (HMI) between electrocardiogram signals and emotional states. The feelings of love, empathy and gratitude produced a clear, harmonious frequency spectrum when recording the electrical activity of the heart with the electrocardiogram. The information of the emotions seemed to be transmitted allover the body. The researchers of HMI also discovered that positive feelings could affect the electromagnetic field of the heart.

I took the habit of giving myself a Reiki self-healing every night before going to sleep. At first, I followed the example self-healing positions that I had learned, and always in the same order. Eventually, Reiki helped me discover meditation, too. Instead of trying not to think of anything while doing Reiki, I focused my attention on the treatment and on the way my hands worked, and remained listening to the sensations of the hands and to what was going on in my mind. I did not consciously try to quiet my mind, but brought my attention to the doing, the listening and the being. Reiki is like meditation with physical routines, such as, for instance, the Chinese qigong exercises, where the mind quiets through the movement and the breath, without any specific attempt to do so. When you repeat the movement and proceed from one movement series to the next, a mental state of flow is born. This also did not seem to involve a need to perform. If I didn't finish the whole series, I wouldn't get the feeling of having somehow failed or that the exercise had been spoiled. Analyzing simply doesn't belong to Reiki. Instead, it felt good that I had done even a little Reiki. Reiki also resembles the mindfulness method, in which one learns to adopt an attitude of acceptance towards the exercises as well as all doing and being. In Reiki, this is not specifically emphasized; it is a natural part of Reiki.

Each time I did self-healing, it seemed to bring something new to the surface. Sometimes it was simply relaxing, at other times, it brought up thoughts and feelings that I would send healing to. I felt that the thoughts and feelings were my own version of the true situation that I could influence and also change, if necessary. I unraveled my own beliefs at the rate that the self-healing brought them up. I undid that onto which I had built, and worked through my own beliefs again. Step by step, a layer at a time, like an onion, I pealed the layers from around me, my own roles and who I was when all the roles had been removed. What would remain? One of my favorite exercises is one that I refer to as the onion pealing exercise, which can be found in Annex 2.

Reiki also seemed to develop my own intuition. A moment on the highway has been particularly ingrained in my mind, when I felt a sting in my belly as if something exciting had just occurred. I decided to be on guard, as I was driving at over 65 mph. I was getting prepared to drive off at a junction and was waiting for the right moment to change lanes. On the bus lane on my right, an old, rusty pick-up passed me. I proceeded to change lanes following the pick-up at the end of the bus lane, when suddenly the pick-up put the brakes on, with the intention of stopping! Even though I had been on guard, I had to push the breaks to the floor. I felt a similar sting in my stomach as before the incident... Luckily I had been on guard! And that time of anticipating things in my stomach would not be the last one. Once I started paying attention to the feeling, it would occur more often. "The attention goes where energy flows..." I often think about the fact that learning to listen to oneself and to one's own reactions takes just as much time as training for an athletic performance or learning a new skill, such as cycling. Admittedly, it is a bit strange to learn such a thing at an adult age, when it feels like these are basic skills that one ought to learn as a child. Or maybe we do know them from birth, but we unlearn them as other things come and replace them? And what would we be capable of, if we were taught intuition and the skill of listening to our inner selves at school?

Almost unawares, the effects of self-healing started showing in my everyday life. I noticed how it became easier for me to look at situations from the outside, to distance myself from what was going on, and to observe myself, and my reactions in the situation. I was also able to predict things. For instance, in situations where things didn't go according to my wishes, I started to sense in my body, how they would evolve. I began to pay attention to my sensations before new situations, and would try to conclude how they would pan out. I might experience a shiver and feeling of tension in my belly before meetings that turned out to be really challenging. If I knew beforehand that there was a difficult situation ahead, it was easier for me to take a deep breath and to distance myself from it, to send Reiki and to see the whole picture. I became more easily sensitized to listening to myself without even consciously trying. It started coming naturally.

When doing Reiki, time and goals seem to loose their importance. There is only this moment and what I am doing right now. That is all. As a result of doing self-healing, my priorities began to change. I also wanted to help others experience what I was experiencing. It is said in some Reiki writings that there is no absolute dividing line as to when one is ready to treat others. However, an indication of sufficient preparedness can be the way one can handle things that arise in one's own daily life. When one is able to receive things objectively and to keep one's peace of mind without letting things get at oneself too much, one can be considered to be at an advanced stage on the spiritual path. Then the mind is clear, open, light, warm and accepting.

Remote healing and Reiki master studies

When learning Reiki, after focusing on the physical body and the healer's personal well-being, the attention is directed toward feelings. Observing feelings will deepen one's self-knowledge and increase the ability to see through one's own views and perhaps illusions, too. Every one of us has assumptions as to how things work and certainly as to how they don't work. Reiki in itself is an example. Surely every Reiki healer will doubt Reiki and its effectiveness at some point. It is part of the process. Also one will question the structures of one's own life, sometimes so strongly that they are completely torn down. It is no longer possible to live according to the same principles as before. Reiki sets in motion various emotions both in the healee and the healer. There is a symbol for dealing with emotions and thoughts in Reiki,

61

called *Sei Hei Ki*. According to Reiki, when drawn on the body, this symbol treats the thoughts and emotions linked to the painful spot, in other words everything behind the pain. *Sei Hei Ki* is often drawn or visualized especially around the heart and head areas. Just like with the *Chokurei* symbol, it must first be internalized and a connection formed through the symbol to one's emotions. One needs to visualize the symbol, watch and think of the symbol as colorful, three-dimensional, vibrating and moving. One has to create a mental image of the things that the symbol will induce. I imagine *Sei Hei Ki* as a soft, bluish, shimmering and translucent wave that sets feelings in motion. When working with emotions, I have often used the Working With Your Emotions Exercise described in Annex 3. It helps identify the topmost feeling on one's mind and to unravel the reasons behind it. Feelings are an indicator. They tell what one ought to be focusing on. Negative feelings express that the direction is wrong and that something ought to be changed. Positive feelings, on the other hand, tell that the direction is right and that more of this is needed. By taking feelings into account, one can form a connection to the underlying thoughts and to one's personal beliefs.

Remote healing, generally speaking, refers to a kind of healing, treatment, wish, meditation or prayer that is deliberately sent by one or more healers to the healee, who is at a distance. In this instance, "at a distance" means further than the reach of hands or other fields that stem from the healer's body. In Reiki, remote healing refers to a treatment that is sent by one or several healers, who have consciously started the remote healing in their mind or drawn the remote healing symbols. In Reiki, there is a specific symbol for starting remote healing and for increasing the treatment's effect: *Hon Sha Ze Sho Nen*. The symbol conjures up images of opening a portal to a timeless space, where the remote healing can occur: time and space don't matter, not even the direction of time. It is possible to heal from a distance, including healees who are far away, and even events that have taken place in the past.

Fig. The Sei Hei Ki- and the Hon Sha Ze Sho Nen symbols.

The symbols can be used like the *Chokurei,* for instance at the beginning of the treatment: One can draw the symbols on both hands and repeat the name of the symbol a couple of times in one's mind. One can visualize how the symbol starts to vibrate. During the treatment, one can also draw the symbol in one's mind to help strengthen the treatment of a particularly painful spot. The symbols can also be used as a mantra: they can be recited in the mind or aloud, when necessary. Furthermore, the *Chokurei* symbol can be used

63

alongside new symbols, and all the symbols can be used together in self-healing, local treatments and remote healing. They can serve to heal the past, the present and the future. Time, place and distance are meaningless; everything happens in this moment. One can imagine moving in a different dimension, at the level of the mind, where the normal cause-and-effect rules don't apply.

Using imagery is helpful for doing Reiki exercises. If imagining things, and using one's senses to create images in front of one's eyes in the mind comes naturally, including imagining sounds, smells, tastes and sensations, then it is easier to dive into the Reiki exercises and see new sides to oneself emerge. It is possible to learn these skills, too. For me, it has always been easy to imagine things. From early on, I have drawn, painted, written fairy tales and poems. Often these were born so that I saw an image in my mind, or as I took a pen in my hand, the story would unfold as if of itself, it already existed in my mind.

Learning Reiki is about learning a new art of perception, it challenges the customary way of thinking and perceiving things. You can imagine being in a space or dimension where time and distance don't apply. Learning Reiki involves, among other things, healing one's own past and future by treating one's timeline with the present as a starting point, moving from either toward the past or the future. In one's mind one can imagine the path as a ribbon with pearls, knots, anything. One can move along the ribbon and treat the knots or examine the pearls.

Healing the timeline was an experience that gave me a feeling of floating. As I healed my timeline, the treatment seemed to go on and on. Suddenly, it seemed to move like a spiral, curling around, bending into many layers, disappearing altogether as if into a different dimension, and yet I could follow it … At times the spiral seemed to cross other spirals, and at other times, it would cross the same spirals again. Sometimes I would discover knots that I tried to open in my mind. Sometimes they would open, melt away, and sometimes they were really stuck. I had different feelings and shivers across my body while I was opening the knots and treating the time spiral. At the end, it felt good to send Reiki to the whole timeline, or actually the time spiral. From the present, I healed the past and the future; everything took place here and now. Understanding this helped also in the learning of remote healing.

Learning Reiki remote healing begins just like the Reiki local healing: at first one has to create one's own treatment routine. A set of actions with which to start the remote healing. After having drawn or visualized the symbols, and recited the personal mantras or phrases that help support the beginning of the treatment, remote healing starts, for instance, by imagining the healee in miniature form between the healer's hands. Healing energy is sent to the healee by visualizing the flow of energy in one's mind. Following one's own sensations, one can focus on those areas where energy isn't flowing as freely or that somehow seem to crave for attention. The treatment is given for as long as one feels that it is needed, or when one perceives that the sense of flow from the hands is slowing down. If, during the session, one gets the feeling that there are some sensations that one needs to share with the healee, then one can do so. However, having sensations is not the intention per se; sending the healing suffices. It is possible to send healing simultaneously to several healees. One can create one's own healing list and write down the names of those that one is sending healing to, and send remote healing directly to that list. The list features the names of the healees, and sending treatment to the list is enough to create a connection to the healees, too. In the treatment, one visualizes the whole group in between one's hands and lets the Reiki flow.

Remote Reiki felt even easier than local healing. It was easier for me to listen to my own emotions and thoughts, and to follow my visions. I was surprised, how strongly the feeling of the area needing treatment would sometimes emerge. There was only a feeling, and when it was shared with the healee, they would confirm that the feeling was correct. I might have visions that the healee would recognize. When receiving distant healing myself, it was easy to get a feeling where there are no limitations of the body. I might feel like I was in a wind tunnel, where I felt flow around me and inside my body. It was a good feeling, a feeling that I was cared for and that I received strength and power.

As an mental image, Reiki is about letting go and acting from the heart. By quieting down the conscious mind, the unconscious, subconscious mind as well as the intuition and the acting from the heart will gain ground. Heart consciousness, in connection with Reiki, refers to the opening up of a new perspective that helps experience things with the heart. It marks the return to a more natural, perhaps also slower, more loving and peaceful way of living and being. Then you are present in a new way to your own heart and to the person who you truly are. It is unconditional, selfless love and acceptance. It is also trust in that everything will always go in the best possible way. All paths are equally right. When you look at a fight between two parties with your heart, you can see how both are sticking to their respective aims and existence. When you let go of the fighting, there is no longer a need to aim for the good and to avoid the bad, but instead you can realize yourself from your innermost self. You come to appreciate that there are no different parties, enemies or opposite points of view, and that we are all one and the same. The heart is the key to unity. By letting go, you will receive all that you have been trying to reach all along.

Daikomio is a symbol related to Reiki's heart consciousness and loving, and it is also referred to as the master symbol of Reiki. It is a symbol that unites everything, like the heart beat or the light that helps recognize the connectedness of everything.

Fig. The Daikomio symbol.

Daikomio assists in processing one's views, truths and fears and helps see the love behind everything. Love is what everything finally returns to. Often the ego will surface strongly when examining feelings. The ego signifies separateness, the role or the roles that each one of us has adopted in this life. Examining and letting go of roles is part of growth, and it is inevitable that through Reiki, roles begin to fall down. In Reiki, roles start to loose their importance one at a time. Roles don't determine who I am, after all. It was even a relief to say: "I am nothing, I am nobody, for no-one…" In other words, I live my life only for myself. The Heart-Mind meditation in Annex 4 is one of my favorite meditations. In this meditation, the focus is directed to your own heart and the feelings that surface just now.

Reiki's heart consciousness course, which marked the beginning of the Reiki teacher training, took place at a time when I craved for energy. My father died in the early fall of 2012. The course was a part of the grieving process for me, dealing with death, loss and letting go. During the course, I worked a lot on the thought of letting go and how I didn't need anything or anybody in order to be me. I am perfect just as I am. In life, one develops various roles, which we use to mirror ourselves and to boost our own ego. If, unintentionally, a role suddenly falls down, we are faced with a crisis of loss. Something changes and we have to let go of it, grieve.

During the course, I felt that I gained contact with my father. He was close to me. Actually, it felt like he was closer than when he was alive, although we had been close. Reiki helped, and gradually from beyond grief, love started to take over. I didn't feel just loss anymore, but instead a feeling of connectedness which I would have liked to share with others, too, immediately. I gained insights about how little we know even about ourselves, and our own lives. I felt that my perspective on everything seemed to widen gradually. I understood, however, that I could not share my view with others, but that everyone had to follow their own path, make their own twists and turns, and live their own lives. All I could do was be present, provide support when necessary and tell what I experience.

I have witnessed wonderful growth stories in Reiki courses. In the courses, people have gained many insights about their own lives. Sometimes the insights have led to the break-up of some relationships and to the birth of new ones. People have also gained insights into the reasons underlying their own health problems and the ways to get rid of them during the courses. Reiki offers help in the midst of changes. I'm grateful for having been able to partake in these.

In this chapter, I have described how I was introduced to Reiki and the kind of issues I encountered as I was learning it. It has been my intention to give an idea of what may occur in the different stages of Reiki studies and how that has affected me. The essential thing about Reiki is what it sets in motion and how that is experienced. For each of us, it will be something different. Therefore, it is not possible to standardize Reiki or energy healing, because each of us needs different things. You can read more about Reiki in L. Johansson's book *Reiki – A Key to Your Personal Healing Power,* P. Miles' book *Reiki: A Comprehensive Guide* or S. McGlinn's book *Reiki, luonnollisen parantamisen menetelmä (available only in Finnish).*

Learning energy healing

My aim is to find the essential core of energy healing. As methods, Bengston's method and Reiki are very different, perhaps even two opposite poles in the spectrum. In Bengston's method, brain activity is accelerated through cycling images. In Reiki, in turn, both the healer's and the healee's mind quiets down. However, in both methods, the brain is "bypassed", in the one, through overload, and in the other, by silencing. In both cases, you work with the mind, rather than focusing on working with and strengthening the energy flowing from the hands. Work on a mental level is of primary importance; the rest will follow, at least, at in the learning stage.

One cannot offer a single, general formula for learning energy healing, but in my experience, the following stages are involved in the development process:

1. The attention is focused on oneself. In Reiki, this is done by means of self-healing, in Bengston's method, by drawing up a personal list.
2. Expanded awareness and emotions. With the different methods, the awareness is expanded to create an emotional state that one tries to maintain during the treatments. In Reiki, it is the feeling of unity and loving, and in Bengston's list, a positive frame of mind.
3. Technique. The method is used to take the attention away from the healing. In Bengston's method, this is done by cycling images, and in Reiki, by letting go of the goal and by listening to the flow of energy and feeling in the hands. The sensation of energy flow can also be increased, for instance with the exercise in Annex 5. There are also other good methods to

increase energy, such as meditation, mindfulness, yoga and Pilates, among others.

4. Mirroring. What is the incentive for continuing to practice? An award that will lead to self-reflection. Such are, for instance, personal insights gained during self-healing and the feedback received from healees regarding the effect of the healing.

I experienced that during the months I practiced energy healing the feeling of flow in my body and warmness in my hands would increase during the healing – both when doing self-healing and when healing others. You can read more about both my own and my healees' experiences in Chapter 6.

CHAPTER 5. What is the essence of energy healing?

"Your vision will become clear only when you look into your own heart."
- Carl Jung (1875-1961)

The things that I have come across in the Reiki and the Bengston method have played an important role in the development of my own energy healing skills. Through the years, a lot has happened, and the healing has also gone through many changes. Just like other people who do energy healing, I have gradually developed my own way of healing. Therefore, I no longer know whether I'm giving Reiki, following Bengston's method or something else. From now on, I will refer to the method that I use simply as energy healing. The way I see it, it is unnecessary, generally speaking, to differentiate between healing methods, that is whether one is healing with Reiki, Bengston's method, Quantum Touch or some other method. Not even the healer can always tell which method they use. Every one of these methods has their own technique that the healer uses to create a state of consciousness from which to heal. Actually, more important than the method is the state created. Some factors often reoccur when creating this state, and I will tell more about it in the following chapter.

Some common features of energy healing

The energy healer creates a connection to the healee using a personal technique. I believe that the following things apply to all energy healing methods:

Who can give energy healing?

- All of us have the capacity to give energy healing; it is an innate skill. Learning different methods can help increase the effect of the healing, but it is not essential.

- Prior to healing others, healers should focus on themselves in order to find their own balance and release the mental obstacles that may stand in the way of the healing.

- Healers can also do self-healing. However, healing given by another person is often said to be more effective.

Does attitude have an effect on the end result?

- Healees can be skeptical about the healing, as long as they are open-minded.

- The healer's intention is often said to have more impact on the healing than the healee's. What is meant by intention is the aim to influence the result of the healing.

  It is common for the healers to express a wish in their mind regarding the result of the healing, which is then released through different methods. Thus, the wishing is not done actively. Hayato et al., among others, describe the healing intention as follows:

  The intention sets the healer's own higher consciousness to the right level, where an energetic, emotional, and spiritual connection prevails with the healee.

How is energy healing done?

- The idea of energy healing is to affect the flow of energy. Energy, here, refers to energy at a mental level, i.e., life energy. In a healthy person, life energy flows well and freely. If the energy channel is blocked and obstructed for some reason, energy healing can help remove the blockage. I will return to the concept of energy and to how science perceives energy, in later chapters. In any case, I can already state here that the energy in question is not the same as the energy referred to in physics.

- In energy healing, the healer "opens" blockages using his or her own method, and one can speak, for instance, "of cleansing of the energy channel", or "of channeling energy from the source". What is essential is that the energy healer has a sense of connection to an exterior source of energy.

- A healer directs energy to the healee in the treatment. Different methods have different ways to strengthen and direct energy. The methods can include such essential features as the location or position of the hands while healing, the use of symbols or mantras that support the healing or a familiarity with meridians and chakras, but none of these are indispensable. There are also methods such as Qigong that focus on strengthening and reviving energy through various spiritual and bodily exercises.

How do energy treatments work and what can they be used for?

- Often physical ailments are associated with – or anchored to – feelings. Sometimes during energy healing, the healee may experience a release of tension and feelings without any clear reason. Emotions can also be associated with memories. The healing can help to see the connection between them and to let go of them altogether.

- Healing may affect and change both the healer's and the healee's attitudes and viewpoint, and bring about a closer connection with other people, and the surrounding world.

- Energy healing can be given locally or remotely. It can be administered to animals, people and plants. It can also be used to heal abstract things, as well as the past and the future.

- It is also possible to use energy healing to "recharge" objects or matter such as, for instance, water or cotton wool.

- Energy healing can be used to heal both the physical and the mental body, that is, the concrete physical body as well as the psychological and sentiments of the mind.

An energy healing session

In the following, I will describe how an energy healing session might unfold in my own treatments. As mentioned before, it is not possible to provide a single standard for energy healing, as every healee and every healing session is different.

Especially when giving your first few energy healing sessions, you tend to pay detailed attention to your own feelings and observations. Because it is a new experience, you deliberate on what you should pay attention to during the treatment. Gradually, with increasing experience, it becomes easier to notice differences and reactions to treatment.

I wrote my own treatment experiences down in order to be able to better follow my observations and my own development. In my treatments there was one factor that was always present in the healing situation: I myself. I wanted to better understand my own influence, and this was indeed a key element in understanding energy healing. When giving a treatment and channeling energy to others, simultaneously the healer receives treatment, too. In a treatment, you act as a channel. You could describe it as water flowing in the pipes; although the majority of the water goes somewhere else, the inside area of the pipe gets wet, too. The treatment affects the healer as well. So I soon noticed, how impossible it was to be in a bad mood and do energy healing at the same time. Inevitably, the emotional state turns positive. I also noticed that it wasn't any problem to give treatments in the evening either, after regular workdays. However tired I might have been at the end of a workday, giving a couple of hours' energy treatment would give enormous amounts of energy to me, too. So much so that once, after returning home from giving the energy treatment, I washed a few windows as well.

I have done energy healing in the most varied environments: in a work place locker room, inside offices, on the beach, in the middle of the road, on the subway, in a car, on accident locations, at fairs, at parties and in peaceful treatment rooms. Energy healing can be given anywhere and anytime. When treatment is needed, the environment is not essential. Rather, the most important thing is that both the healer and the healee experience the environment as suitable for healing. In an ideal situation, I would, of course, prefer to give a treatment in a peaceful treatment room, where we can relax without unnecessary interruptions. However, in my experience, it is not really necessary to create any special circumstances before starting the session, such as creating a more peaceful environment with music, to quiet yourself down, or to meditate. Occasionally, I have "cleansed" the space on a mental level, if I've had a feeling that the energy of the room wasn't conducive to healing. This kind of feeling can arise, for instance, from an argument that has taken place inside the room. This way, the surroundings can offer a cozier space in which to give healing. Surely, the energy will "flow" simply as one starts to do energy healing. Each healer will naturally create his or her own "rituals" in preparation for the healing session. Personally, I have meditated or done self-healing before starting the treatment, if I have had a feeling that the upcoming energy healing session will be challenging. This has quieted my mind, and freed myself, as well as the session, from a goal-oriented attitude – opening the channel to function as well as possible right from the start.

It is easiest to give local treatment to a client lying on a treatment table or sitting on a chair, wearing his or her normal daily clothes. The client can also lie on a sofa or bed, or even stand, whichever is the easiest way to arrange the treatment situation. Usually, I will ask the client to take a comfortable position and to relax; that is all that the client needs to do. The client can let his or her thoughts wander anywhere. You don't have to be quiet; it is okay to talk. The client can, however, observe their reactions and sensations, and what the treatment brings up. Often the conversation can be meaningful, and it can assist in the opening of a "blockage". Mostly, I commence the energy healing for the whole body from the head to the feet on the front side, and then proceed from the backside up. In the beginning, I would start a local treatment in the same way as self-healing, in other words by drawing Reiki symbols on the hands and by wishing the highest possible energy for the healee that they are able and ready to receive. After having given treatments for some time, I no longer felt the need to draw symbols on my hands; the treatment seemed to start immediately with the simple thought of starting it. Also, in the treatment, I always include the words "the energy healing becomes available for my healee in the best possible way" and "immediately" rather than sometime later…. I have also observed that unconsciously, as I start the treatments, I take a deep breath in and a deep breath out. When doing this, I simultaneously feel shivers in my body. Often I also visualize, how the energy flows in from the top of my head (the crown chakra) into my heart (the heart chakra), and from there into the hands and feet "with the full width of the channel", filling me entirely. I set my hands over the spot to be treated or touch it lightly, whichever might feel best, and then I simply let the "energy" flow in my mind. I visualize how my client receives exactly that what they need. I experience being in touch with my own inner self, while I also experience being just a channel. At this point, I often set out to go through Bengston's list. I cannot influence the end result in any other way but by directing the flow of energy toward the desired target. I only act as a guide and express a wish as to the end result. While giving treatments, I often have the same feeling as when doing self-healing: a pleasant, light feeling, a sense of relaxing, like a flow inside and a tickling feeling in the middle of my brain.

DOES ENERGY HEALING WORK?

CHAPTER 6. Energy healing experiences

Everything happens at the right moment. Be patient.
-Anonymous

In this chapter, I will share my own energy healing experiences and describe how the treatments have changed. I will also describe my clients' experiences and a few treatment cases.

Different types of sensory experiences

In energy healing, the healers learn to be energy mediators, simply channels for the healing and nothing else. At the level of thought, the healer can express a wish as to the result of the treatment and visualize it as fulfilled, but the healer cannot typically direct or personally affect the healing process. There is no need to feel, be or do anything. You are simply a channel and let go of the target. As you begin to give treatments, the most challenging thing is quieting down your own conscious mind. The conscious mind, or *ego*, argues that the treatment must be felt in some way and that it cannot work, as it cannot possibly be so easy... You ought to be able to tell where the problem lies, and be able to focus on treating that particular ailment. In spite of this, I decided to give energy healing a chance and to see what would happen. At first, the treatments would involve mainly listening to and observing my own reactions, sensations and thoughts. I listened in the same way as when doing self-healing, that is to what the treatment would bring up in me. The first few times, I acted exactly as taught: I drew Reiki symbols in my hands, recited the initial words in my mind to support the treatment, and proceeded to give the treatment. I couldn't feel much else than heat, sometimes more from one side than the other. I was attentive to possible differences, and to my own reactions and thoughts during the treatment. Later on, I realized that I unconsciously focused my attention on my thoughts and reactions, which gradually started as if to unravel a ball of yarn including my own thought patterns and assumptions, one at a time. My attention was not focused on the actual treatment, but on my thoughts and experiences.

In the early stages, I barely had any expectations regarding the treatment. I was skeptical. At most, I would expect that the patient would get a sensation of heat from my hands warming them, nothing more. When my client would report experiencing more than just heat, I would be surprised, and would explain the many sensations as being products of the mind. The mind can create miracles. Some of the most challenging phases in learning energy healing involved letting go of my expectations and of my own ego, as well as of my role as a healer. Little by little, my mind started to quiet down and relaxed when giving treatments. Increasingly, the conscious mind would step out of the way of the treatments. It started to let go of targets and goals, and stopped trying. Various visualization exercises, as well as mindfulness and self-awareness exercises, in which you are simply present in the now, listening within, helped in the process. Along with these exercises, the feeling grew that I was personally acting as a channel for the treatment. Letting go of control and just being present in the moment is liberating, and it was as if the treatment moved to a different level.

Heat is naturally the first thing that you notice when giving and receiving treatments. The experience of heat can vary in different parts of the body, and you can gain a sense of which place to heal. When giving healing, I personally start by paying attention to the differences in the heat radiating from the body. The heat, and the sensations in the hands would change. I could also have sensations in some part of my own body, which would turn out to be the same as my healee's. For instance, after having treated a client with neck and leg problems, I would leave the room limping and with a stiff neck... The ailments would, however, always disappear within a couple of minutes after the treatment, and they didn't really seem to be in my body. Due to these sensations, I started doing "grounding exercises" in my mind after the treatments to help getting rid of the "echo pain": I would visualize that water washes away all my healee's pains, sensations and ailments, and I would even wash my hands with real running water after the healing session. I might also walk outside barefooted, preferably by the seaside.

I had the feeling that as I began a treatment, I would establish a connection with a common "energy field" or information. During the treatment, both the healee and I were connected through the field and might have similar sensations. I began to learn: my own sensations and the type of ailment in question seemed to correlate. Different types of ailments would feel different, for instance a cut wound felt different from a road rash. A broken hand felt different from a sprained hand. However, I would naturally leave the making of the diagnosis to the professionals. Still now, I ask my clients to go to the doctor first, if necessary, to have the situation assessed, while I'm also happy to treat them afterwards, in case that is what they want. The treatments gradually started to change, and I began to have more and more sensations with colors, images and shapes during the healing. There was a particularly memorable moment a couple of years ago, when I started seeing magnificent, deep colors in my minds eye during the treatments. At first there was a dark, deep and simultaneously bright lilac color. At the same time, there was movement, sometimes undulating, at other times rotating and flowing. Mostly, the lilac would occur in the area of the head, but sometimes I would see it in other places, too. It seemed to tell me where to treat, since it would often appear exactly in the places that were in pain. When I paid attention to the colors, they would increase. There was a deep, bright turquoise that seemed to mostly show up around the neck. In the area of the stomach, there was a reddish, orange and yellowish color. As an interesting observation, I noticed that the colors were the same and in similar locations as how chakras are often described. Furthermore, I might often see a revolving movement, as if there was a whirl of energy in the areas of the chakras, stronger in some places than in others. When I observed the color, it seemed to expand and to get deeper still. At the same time, the focus on the actual doing would disappear. It was particularly interesting that often my healees would see the same colors and movements as I.

Sometimes during treatments, I might see images or situations as if in a flash. At first, I didn't mention these to my patients, as I considered them to be coincidences and figments of my own imagination. However, on one occasion, I decided to tell about it, as I thought that even from a research point of view, it would be interesting to know what my client experienced at that very moment. As I was treating the healee's head area, I suddenly saw a blond woman's face and asked myself who she was. In my mind, the answer came as Annikki or Anneli - a name starting with Ann. The healee told me about her deceased friend, whose name was Annelise. It felt as if the friend had come to provide support for my client, just like she had supported and been there for her friend at the time when she was dying.

I have also noticed several times that just as I was thinking about something, my client would start talking about the same thing. Once during a treatment, my client's deceased husband and mother came to my mind, and at the moment when I was about to ask her about them, she started describing her summer cottage that she had last visited in the company of her husband and mother!

Often when doing a whole body treatment, there is a sense of timelessness, of another dimension, that both the healer and the healee occupy. The body's boundaries – both my own and the healee's – seem to dissolve, and it is difficult to tell where I end and the healee begins. The feeling is that it is not a body that I am treating, rather the treatment happens on an entirely different level. It is often a surprise for both to realize how long a treatment has taken. The treatment might have taken almost 1,5 hours, yet it feels like the time passed could have been only 20 minutes.

All the experiences that I have had while healing have been a great addition to the treatments. Often it has felt like the experiences of both parties involved have lifted the treatment to a new level. Energy healing, in combination with relaxing and conversation, initiates an inner process in the patient.

What can be treated?

Energy healing can be applied to practically any situation, ailment or state. I have used energy healing for many ailments, such as stomach pain, throat ache, ear pain, head ache, migraine, wounds and sprains. I have used it as a support in the case of many diseases and illnesses, and used it to treat tumors as well. Anything can be treated. Usually I will treat the head area first and then move on to the problem area itself or give a full body treatment. In some energy healing methods, the body is scanned through, and specific "hot spots" are searched, which radiate an unusual heat or a sense of needing treatment. In Reiki, in turn, you act as a channel for the treatment and let go of the target. Naturally, I wish well when giving healing and hope that the healing will reach the very spot where it is needed, and to help in the best possible way, but then I let go of the target and don't actually provide the healing but act instead as a channel.

If the need for healing is acute, such as in the case of a wound, I set my hands directly over the wound without treating the head area first. It seems that healing has a quicker effect on acute ailments than on ones that have developed over a longer period of time. For instance, a headache seems to heal faster than a long-standing neck pain. William Bengston also stated that the effect of healing is faster in acute cases, and furthermore, that it is faster with younger than with older people. I treat children in the same way as adults, but a shorter treatment time seems to suffice with children. According to Bengston, the reason is

84

that with children, the ego is not an obstacle to healing. Children mostly want treatment only when there is a real need for it, and say immediately when it is enough. It is the same with animals, too: animals don't stay in care after they have had enough. Most animals enjoy the treatment very much and are good at relaxing. The effects of the treatment also seem to show faster with animals, as is the case with children.

Plants, too, fare much better when they receive energy healing. Clients, whose homes I had visited to give regular treatments, told me about flowers that they were about to throw away, but had started freshening up and even blossoming in a room where healing had taken place before. One flower, an orchid that I purchased for my therapy room, was amazing. It blossomed non-stop for almost a year: on the little stem, there were big flowers all the time. Then it would take a couple of weeks' break and start developing a new sprout again. The effect of energy healing on plants has also been researched. In the case of plants, it is easier to exclude different variables that affect the healing. Doctor Bernard Grad from McGill University in Montreal studied the effect of energy healing on barley seeds in the 1960s. The seeds were planted in pots, and they were watered with a saline solution that was known to slow down the germination and growth of seeds. In a double blind experiment, the seeds were divided into two groups. The first group of seeds was watered with the saline solution, which had been given energy healing for 15 minutes. The other group was watered with untreated water. The people who had watered the seeds didn't know which group received which water. The seeds that were watered with the treated water grew faster and 25% heavier than those that had been watered with untreated water. They also showed a higher level of chlorophyll content. The experiment was repeated several times, with similar results. Doctor Robert Miller has also conducted a number of experiments related to energy healing. He has studied, among others, the effect of energy healing on the growth speed of plants and discovered that the growth is speeded up considerably as a result of the healing. The speeding up of the plants' growth rate has also been found by the Spindrift group, which studied the effect of prayer. According to the group, the plants that had been prayed for always grew faster and were healthier than those that hadn't been prayed for, although otherwise, the plants' circumstances were the same. The results were the same regardless of the distance from which the prayers took place.

Especially at the beginning, the healing sessions were about learning and figuring things out for me as well as for my healees. Every healing session felt different, even when healing the same person on subsequent sessions. At first, I would mostly treat my close circle of family and friends. Naturally, each person approached the energy healing in their own way, some doubting, some giving it a try with an open mind. Sometimes a single healing session sufficed to set something new in motion and to strengthen the move toward in a desired direction. Also, I would often feel that the mere mention of my healee's name would make my hands feel warm, and make the treatment start as remote healing. Still, this often happens. In addition, I also noticed that it was easier for me to send remote healing to a person, whom I had given local healing to at least once. It felt like the connection had already been created during the local healing session.

With the actual remote healing sessions that are set in advance, I tend to agree on a mutually convenient time with my client. However, not even this is really necessary; the treatment can be sent, and the healee can receive it when it best suits them. A joint time is, however, often agreed upon, so that both the healer and the healee will put aside the time for the healing session and observe their respective sensations. Especially when I wanted to observe my own and my healee's experiences, it was good to set a joint time. Preparing for remote healing depends a lot on the healer, and each healer will provide his or her own instructions. Some healers may organize the remote healing through a live connection, while others may just agree on a time when the healing will take place.

At the beginning of the remote healing session, I ask my patient to withdraw into a quiet space, where they can relax and listen to their own sensations. I will also withdraw into my space and perform my own routines, which I use to start the treatment. What has surprised me in remote healing is how strongly I feel the treatment, as if the patient was by my side. Usually I would feel cold shivers at first, as if I was standing in the middle of a stream that flowed from my head to the feet, and I might also feel tickling in the middle of my brain. The feeling is pleasant and relaxed. Many people who have experienced my remote healing sessions have reported similar experiences, and often they have fallen asleep after the treatment.

Many are surprised that the remote healing works so well. As a notion, remote healing challenges many people's own thinking and views. I will return to how remote healing can be explained in later chapters.

My own and my clients' experiences of energy healing

Among the first experiences mentioned by my clients, especially on initial treatments, is good relaxation. "Pleasant calming and quieting down, for once my mind quieted down in a good way, without any effort", commented one of my clients. What is also often mentioned is the warmth or even heat in the area being treated. Someone might feel the effect of the treatment as tingling or cold shivers, instead of heat. When the healee feels cold shivers or a sense of a flow in the body, sometimes even momentary pain, which then passes, I myself feel that, too. As if the flow started from my hands and streamed through the whole body of my healee. When I see colors and movement while healing, often the healee will also report having seen colors, movement and undulating behind closed eyes. The healing seems to set something in motion and this can be completely different at different times, even when treating the same person. Mostly, the healee feels pleasure, like after having slept well or travelled to another dimension. Also, the sense of time disappears and many are surprised by how much time has actually passed. One of my clients compared her feeling to the way you feel after a hard workout: a long-standing tension in the muscles is released and the feeling is "beat".

My clients seek help for health issues and for their own well-being, and to support inner growth. I often get feedback for pain relief, or for the pain having disappeared entirely; for a better ability to cope, lifted spirits and a general easing of symptoms, whether related to a long-standing illness or a more acute ailment. Gratitude, increased clarity, seeing the order of importance of things or a change of priorities, an increase of positivity and an advent of love in life are among the experiences reported by my clients. Longer-term-effects of energy healing on my clients' life can be described as spiritual growth, and for many, life has taken on an entirely new and even surprising direction, as energy healing has brought increased self-confidence, trust in one's own abilities and the courage to let go. Among other effects mentioned are a sense of speedier recovery, a decrease of stress and anxiety, an easing of emotional states, a feeling of peacefulness and well-being, an easing of falling asleep, a deepening of sleep, an increase in the amount of sleep, and a better frame of mind.

In the table below, my own subjective healing experiences are listed in the context of specific treatment cases. Often, I give my client a full body treatment, i.e., I begin by treating the head area, and then proceed to heal the body, with a special focus on the areas that the healee themselves wishes to have treated. Because the body is a whole, often one can find that a painful spot is connected to a completely different place in the body. The length of a treatment varies from about 10 minutes in the case of local treatments to full body treatments that may take over an hour. Clearly, the acute ailments seem to be the fastest to treat and to react, whereas with ailments that have developed over a long time, the effect can be seen more slowly. For instance, an acute headache reacts quickly to a treatment in comparison with tumors that have developed over a long period of time. If the healee is on some medication, I might notice it like a curtain of fog between us. It feels like I can't get a proper connection to the healee. In such cases, I follow my intuition and give a longer treatment especially to the head.

Treatment case	Length of treatment	Experiences
Headache	ca. 10 min, 1x	Healer: Strong sense of heat in the hands. Healee: Feeling of heat on the head area. Other: When the sense of heat in the hands subsides, the pain disappears, too.
Migraine	ca. 10-15 min	Healer: The area of pain feels clearly heated; often the heat can also be felt in my own head. Healee: The same as when treating a headache. Other: If the treatment is given right after noticing the first symptoms, it will be shorter in duration or the attack won't start at all.
Sprains	ca. 10-15 min, until the feeling of heat and pain subsides	Healer: The sprain is felt as heat. Healee: The pain subsides. Other: Speedier recovery?
Fractures	Several times at intervals as short as possible	Healer: Heat in the area to be treated. Heat and throbbing, or dull ache in the palms while giving the treatment. Healee: Heat in the treated area. Other: Throbbing or dull ache during initial treatments; the heat lasts longer.
Wounds	Depending on the size of the wound	Healer: The type of wound can be felt in the hand (cut, deep wound, road rash, or sting). More difficult wounds can be felt at a further distance than smaller ones. Healee: Throbbing in the wound, the pain recedes. Other: The type of wound is felt the strongest on the first treatment, less so on further treatments.
Asthma	When the symptoms are felt	Healer: Strong heat radiating especially from the healee's chest area. Healee: Mucus is released during the treatment. Other: The healee's breath moves more smoothly toward the end of the treatment.

Treatment case	Length of treatment	Experiences
Tumors (benign, malignant)	Locally. Benign: several months, malignant: faster reaction.	Healer: Feeling of heat in the palms. Healee: Heat in the treated area. Other: Mostly they grow first and then disappear. Malignant: the heat emanating from the treated area feels really hot, it is not possible to hold the hand on it. The heat quickly subsides. On the next treatment, the situation is repeated. More frequent and shorter treatments seem to be better.
Fibromyalgia	Full body treatment 1-2 times/ month over several months	Healer: Feeling that the energy doesn't flow everywhere. For instance, around the head area, there is a good flow, but there is a blockage around the neck. Different chakras have a different feel: the top ones feel strongly, then comes a feeling of blockage, and the lower ones feel cooler. Healee: Feels the energy flow and the place where there is a possible blockage during the treatment.
Parkinson's	As much as possible	Healer: Feeling as if thoughts had drifted somewhere outside, and that remote healing should be given rather than treating just the head area. Healee: Strong feeling of heat, relaxed sensation.
Stomach aches, IBD	Acute cases: 1-2 times, More chronic cases: regularly	Healer: Strong feeling of heat in the hands Healee: The heat is felt especially in the painful areas
Grief	Until the feeling eases	Healer: The healee's head feels hot, also the chest is unusually hot. The stomach area is also hot. Healee: The healer's hands emanate heat that feels even burning hot at times.

Client A, 70+ years old, diagnosed with Parkinson's disease. The right shoulder blade is aching.

While treating my client, I didn't know about him having been diagnosed with Parkinson's disease. My intention was to treat the aching shoulder blade; it was preventing the hand from moving normally. I started the treatment from the area of the head, as I often do in other cases, too. While being treated, the area of the head, the so-called crown chakra, did not feel hot like it usually does; it felt as if the crown chakra was blocked. Instead, around it, I could feel quite a lot of heat. It felt like the area that I should treat was somewhere around the head rather than inside it. As an exceptional measure, I also sent him remote healing simultaneously while giving a local energy treatment, because I sensed that it might be helpful. I often draw remote healing symbols in my mind also while giving local healing, but now I did the same as when giving remote healing, although my client was right beside me. The edge of the right shoulder blade, which was painful, was clearly emanating heat. Also, I had the feeling that there was something in the knee that needed treating, and that the back, the hip and the pelvis required more attention. I told my client about my sensations, and as it turned out, he had had difficulties walking lately. As I was giving the treatment, an image also came to my mind of a little, blond boy running in a hayfield in the countryside in blue knickerbockers. His mother was calling him with a scarf around her head, in a long skirt and wearing an apron. I told how I was feeling and the image from the countryside seemed to be his childhood scenery, also he could easily recognize the knickerbockers. As a result of a single treatment, the pain in the right shoulder eased at least temporarily and he could lift his arm higher than before. The healee was also much perkier and seemed to be more present.

Later, I told my healee about the feeling I had while treating the area of the head: it was as if what needed treating was located somewhere completely different than inside the head. It was then that I learned about the Parkinson's diagnosis. Unfortunately he lived so far away that we could not continue the local treatments, and I couldn't rely on remote healing yet at the time. Local healing felt more meaningful and timely to me then.

I found out later that Parkinson's disease is the result of the slow destruction of the nerve cells in an area of the brain that controls movement. The reason for it is not known. The destruction of the nerve cells leads to the decrease in dopamine, which in turn leads to the neural pathways regulating the movements getting damaged. For me, the description explained my sensation of the crown chakra being blocked. What I have retained particularly clearly in my mind from this treatment, is how the area to be treated can actually be somewhere entirely different, and is maybe only at times in the place where I am treating.

Client B, 50+ years old, fibromyalgia. Back pains.

One of my clients, who suffered from back pains, came to my care after her doctor had suggested Reiki treatment as a support to medical care. Usually, in the first healing sessions, I focus on treating the head area, because I have the feeling that this is what is needed. The healing might be about enabling an opening and about establishing a connection. This time, immediately upon laying my hands over my client's head, I felt my hands turn burning hot and as if a sucking had begun and had drawn "energy" from my hands. It felt like there was an immediate connection. The same continued with the area of the throat and chest: a warmness, even heat, and "sucking". At about the level of the waist, the feeling changed: the sucking stopped completely, and so did the feeling of heat. As if there was an obstacle, a blockage, through which nothing could pass. No heat could be felt anymore. My hands felt the same as when I started the treatment: very warm. I also treated the knees and the soles of the feet. The feeling was the same: as if there was a blockage somewhere higher up, because the flow couldn't reach them, either. On the backside, around the middle of the back, the same blockage could be felt. In the lower back, there was no sensation of heat or sucking, but the upper back would warm up again. Before I had the time to describe my sensations, my client told me that she felt as if there was a blockage or lock in her back. I healed the area of the blockage, with one hand over the upper back and the other hand over the lower back, with the idea of helping induce the flow, and of "melting" the blockage.

In the course of the following healing sessions, the obstacle in the back seemed to gradually dissolve and the warmth to spread to the lower back, too. The flow was, at times, really strong: as I was treating the feet, the client felt how the flow passed through the whole body all the way to the top of the head so that even the hair would seem to rise. Stress felt like a sizeable factor in the client's condition. Sometimes, work-related stress would cause back pain to recur more strongly, and the blockage in the back to be felt more clearly. During the following months, however, the client's state began to stabilize. I also did the Reiki activations to my client and taught her to do self-healing. This seemed to be very helpful to her.

I have also treated another person suffering from fibromyalgia. In her case, my experience was the same as before: first, a strong sense of flow in the head area, and a feeling of heat in my hands from the very start of the first treatment. This time, too, a blockage could be felt: in her case, around the neck. Also, the blockage would gradually "melt" away during the treatments. I had the feeling that both of my clients were very sensitive, spiritual people, as if their body could not keep up with the pace.

Client C, 70+ years old, migraine. An attack is just about to start.

A client whom I was treating had the feeling of a pending migraine attack. She saw zigzag patterns and knew from experience that the feeling was like it often was just before the onslaught of an attack. Usually she kept the medication at hand, just in case, but this time she had forgotten it. As I started the healing, I immediately had a feeling of pressure on my own forehead, which turned out to be the same spot as where my client felt pain at that very moment. I felt a dull ache on my forehead, and in my hands, I could feel heat in the same spot as on my client's forehead. Having treated for some time, the dull ache disappeared from my forehead and the feeling subsided from my hands. My client commented that she felt better, but the following hours would tell, whether the attack would start anyway. Later on she told me that the attack had not started on that occasion.

My client comes to me for treatment regularly on a monthly basis, and during the individual sessions, I have noticed that I can recognize whether she has taken medication or not. If she has taken medication, I feel like I'm healing through a curtain of fog, and getting the session started takes longer, as if there were problems in establishing a connection. My client has suffered from migraine for decades and she told me that since the beginning of the regular monthly treatments, the number of days with migraine has decreased, and that she has also been able to cut down on medication. In addition, she has experienced that her spirits have lifted and turned more positive, and considers this to be thanks to the energy healing sessions.

In my experience, headache and migraine feel very similar from a healer's perspective. I might recognize the spot with the most intense pain in my own body, which helps give the treatment. When the feeling disappears from my own body, it usually disappears from my healee's body as well.

Client D, 40+ years old. Spiritual development.

Energy healing sessions can be very different even if they are given within a short intervals. My client had previously attended Reiki 1 and 2 courses, but she had never personally had a Reiki treatment. The client had also given treatments to her close circle of family and friends, but felt that it wasn't her life mission: she considered Reiki mostly as a tool for self-healing. The treatments varied a lot. The first time, she had emotions across the board.

The treatment started with a strong feeling of fear, which she experienced as being linked to the fact that through the treatment, you get more closely in touch with yourself. The fear might have been caused by her resistance to change. Occasionally, she would get strong cold shivers and a feeling that in the area of the stomach, something had turned over. As the treatment went on, she felt that the tensions around the body would release, and by the end she was finally able to relax.

The following treatment was much more visual and physically peaceful. My client related a feeling of warmth, which could be felt in my hands as really hot, but relaxing. She had a feeling of great weight and even a sense of being paralyzed. It was even difficult for her to move any part of the body. At the same time, she reported visualizing changing colors, movement and undulating, and gradually images of different forest animals and other figures. What made this particularly interesting was that I would also see flashes of the same images. At first, I had the feeling that there were other figures around, too. Then, for a brief moment, in the corner of my eye, I perceived a small, greenish gray man with curly hair and a beard. I was astonished, and at that very moment, the images disappeared.

Initially, my client came to my healing sessions out of interest, but also to gain a better understanding of herself and perhaps of her life mission. She wanted to know what she was truly meant to do. For my client, the treatments were an opportunity to focus herself in the midst of busy days, and to listen to what might arise from within. In the treatments, things surfaced that until then, she had only bypassed without working them through, but that, however, had stuck to her body. Gradually, she started going increasingly in the direction of the life that she had always wanted to live.

I have noticed how my clients' insights during the treatments will also affect me. Although I heal someone else, I receive healing myself, too. When my client relates that they have noticed being really happy during the healing session, and that actually they don't need anything more in their life, and that all is well just as it is, I feel how words, too, are energy and stem from somewhere deep. My clients need the energy of those words to create such a reality for themselves, but at the same time, they are also meant for me. I might have just been pondering on similar themes and my client reinforces my thinking. Often one can only wonder at how synchronously things occur!

Client E, ca. 50 years old. Chronic flu, stomach pains.

Client E is passionate about yoga and has also personally attended Reiki courses. Although you might give energy healing, it is also good, from time to time, to seek support from others for your own well-being. My client needed healing because she had begun to suffer from stomach pains. She had tried all kinds of diets to no avail and gone to the doctor's several times. When the doctor had finally started discussing gastroscopy, E became scared and decided that the pain had to come to a stop. Also, my client's well-being was eaten up by recurring cases of flu.

Already on the first healing session, I could see that my client tended to her and to others' well-being. It felt like the treatment got to an immediate start: my hands warmed up and turned blotchy, and I began to see colors and undulating movement behind closed eyes. The first few healing sessions became strongly centered on the sensations as I treated the head area. Both she and I experienced strongly the warmth, as well as the lilac color and undulating movement, which could also be seen in the following sessions, with the movement changing each time: spinning, undulating, dividing from the center or showing as a unified pattern. When treating the hands, she had a feeling of deepening, falling, loosing track of the body's outline, sometimes a sense of weightlessness or a feeling that the whole body was spinning in the room. I couldn't feel the stomach area in any particular way while healing, but my patient felt as if her innards were put back in place in a different order. I could feel the soles of the feet very strongly. It felt as if a line had run from them across the whole body, and I visualized sending energy along that channel. The stomach pains disappeared after the first few healing sessions without returning again, and her face started regaining a rosy color.

The following treatments were focused on healing the head and various ailments. It felt like the ailments were in line: the stomach aches having eased, the next time, surprisingly it was the area of the lungs that called for most healing due to its allergy and asthma symptoms. Then we moved on to treat the back that had been injured at youth, the removed ovaries and the grief at the loss of close ones. When one layer had been treated, a new one would surface. I didn't want to know which ailment requiring healing was the most acute one. I would usually be able to easily recognize which are needed energy while healing. Sometimes I would be surprised by my discoveries. I might find an aching toe, which would turn out to be an ailment stemming from childhood and which had now suddenly started to ache again. Sometimes it felt like someone had intentionally placed random ailments into my client just to see if I could find what the issue was this time…

Occasionally, the healing sessions were very deep experiences for me, too, as a healer. In addition to feeling, at times, like the whole room was spinning, at other times it felt like I had lost my body entirely. The body's boundaries seemed to disappear, and I could no longer feel my hands. Sometimes I would actually be startled and check whether my patient was there anymore, either. It was as if both of us were bodiless, pure energy.

In the year following the start of the healing sessions, my client came down less with the flu than before and felt that her well-being had lifted to the level that she desired.

Client F, 60 years old, fractured wrist

Client F's hand was fractured as she fell down in slippery weather in the winter cold. As the pain in the hand didn't seem to ease on the day, she went to the doctor's, who took an X-ray and discovered a fracture in the wrist. Wearing a cast for several weeks was depressing, and as she had previously had problems with the healing of a fracture, additional care was not a bad idea.

At first, I treated her a couple of times a week, during which time the swelling of the hand gradually went down. In the beginning, while I was treating, she would often have a throbbing feeling in the fracture area. I myself would feel pressure in my own hand in the corresponding place.

Already a month after the fall, the hand felt almost normal and well healed. When the cast was removed, the doctor was surprised at how good the hand looked. The hand also worked quite well immediately after the cast was taken off.

Client G, child, road rash

A child had a road rash as a result of falling down on a bicycle, with the skin crumpled over an area of 2 inch x 2 inch. The wound was aching. I treated over the wound, holding my hand a few inches over it. The child had a burning feeling in the wound when I started the treatment, and the aching continued. I could sense the size of the wound in my palm as a feeling of pressure. When I moved my hand further away, the wound could still be felt easily a dozen inches away. The ideal distance from which to heal seemed to be two or three inches away. In my mind, I imagined how the energy was flowing into the wound and healing it. The feeling of pressure gradually turned into a sense of throbbing, the child told me that the pain had eased and that now he could only feel heat and throbbing.

I healed for 15 minutes, and gradually the throbbing and heat subsided. The child commented that he could no longer feel the pain and went on to play. The wound healed well.

Client H, about 60 years old, remote healing for shoulder pain

I have often experienced that it is easier to give remote healing for a client if I have previously given them local treatment. However, local treatment is not a prerequisite for remote healing to work. For me this was proved by the remote healing session that I gave to a patient who suffered from shoulder pain. For years, she had occasionally had aches around one shoulder and shoulder blade, which she suspected had started from poor working positions at the computer, in other words the ailment was a so-called "mouse shoulder". Many different treatments had been tried for the ailment, including cortisone shots, but it would recur after having been absent for various lengths of time.

We agreed with my client on a joint appointment, during which I would send her remote healing while she would withdraw to her own private space to rest for a while and pay attention to her feelings.

At the time agreed, I performed my normal routines to start the remote treatment. In my mind, I visualized my client and how I would send her the treatment. I felt a cold shiver pass through my whole body and had the feeling that the treatment had begun. I visualized how I would send remote healing to my client's head, neck and shoulder area. My attention was especially focused on the right shoulder and the area of the shoulder blade. I also felt a stinging ache and pressure in my own right shoulder. I sent the healing especially to the area of the shoulder and listened to how it felt, and whether the feeling of pain was changing in some way. The stinging feeling in my own shoulder stopped and the sense of pressure turned into heat, which gradually cooled down and stabilized. I continued treating for a while yet, until, after about half an hour, I felt that the sense of energy flow in my body and hands gradually stopped.

After the remote treatment, I talked with my client. She reported having felt heat around the shoulder and having fallen asleep probably 10 minutes after the start of the treatment. The shoulder didn't feel sore. She agreed to report how the situation would develop: whether the pain will return, and if it will, in what form. A few months after the remote healing session, I talked with my client when she came to my course. The shoulder pain had not returned. Almost four years have passed since that remote healing session, and the pain has still not recurred.

A summary of the experiences

In my experience, if you seek support for the healing of a long-term ailment, you will gain the most benefit from having a regular treatment at the interval of two weeks to a month. The length of the treatment depends on the ailment and on what you want from the treatment. A regular treatment is about focusing your attention on your own well-being. It is a moment that allows you to discharge all the things that you continuously and unwillingly gather within. Many of the people who come to my treatments are also energy healers, and heal others as well as themselves. In order to be able to heal others, one has to take care of one's own well-being. Acute ailments and ailments born in a short space of time seem to react faster to healing. Conditions that are born over a longer period would also seem to require longer treatment. This is, however, not always the case. Sometimes a single treatment can provide help for long-term ailments, such as in the case of the remote healing of a shoulder blade described above.

I have found it to be most helpful when a client themselves wants to learn the method, as this means that they will take a stronger responsibility over their own well-being. An observation about my clients: 85% of those who have attended my healing sessions at least three times have become interested within one year after the start of my treatments in learning another method related to spiritual growth, or learned to give energy healing themselves. Also Dr. Daniel J. Benor tells in the summary of his research on energy healing that energy healing is often related to an increase in spiritual consciousness. Energy healing would also seem to have a connection with one's own life management skills and the decision to do something themselves. In the course of one year following the Reiki course, those who had attended it reported, among others, of having changed jobs and entire career directions, ended relationships, got rid of addictions (cigarette, coffee, sweets) and otherwise increased their own well-being. Naturally, the course wasn't the starting point for change for everybody, but a part of a change that was already underway.

A treatment would not always seem to immediately affect the ailment that is primarily being treated. For instance, while treating someone with a stomach ache, they might first report about the relaxing and easing of stress symptoms, leading to the stomach ache to ease, too. Energy healing heals as a whole. It is not even necessary to touch, or even occupy the same space as the client; the treatment can also be given from a distance. In some cases, the symptoms may get worse at first before starting to get better. Bengston found the same in his mouse studies, where the mice's tumors seemed to keep growing at first, before they started to decrease and dry up. The worsening of the symptoms has, however, been very short term.

Even though every healing session is different, the start of my own treatments often follows the same formula: I close my eyes, breathe deeply, bring my attention to my breath and follow its course. Then I widen my attention to encompass the entire area of the head, often to the forehead. Then I observe the feeling on the top of the head and in the hands and feet, and feel how love fills the heart and the state for healing is created. If I give local healing, I set my hands over the area to be treated and channel healing while simultaneously observing with eyes closed the vibration, changing colors and other sensations.

During the treatment, my own spirits are lifted, too. I have never started a treatment unwillingly, but I might have been tired otherwise. In the course of the treatments, my own spirits are lifted as well, as if I, too, receive healing. If I give several treatments in succession, I have felt the need to zero in, calibrate, and ground myself between treatments. This is mostly a state of mind, where I consciously set the issues related to the previous treatment aside to avoid transferring anything on to the next client. Often, I perform the grounding physically, too, usually by washing my hands under running water.

With children and animals, the treatment seems to work faster than with adults. Often it is explained that at first, an energy treatment quiets down the conscious mind and the ego. The ego fights back and claims that "the treatment and recovering are impossible", and argues why they don't work. However, children and animals don't have an ego standing in the way of healing like adults. Children and animals are open and receive the healing when they need it without expectations and beliefs. Thinking objectively, I cannot take another stand here than to state that in the case of children and animals, the treatment seems to work faster.

CHAPTER 7. Melli

Listen to your heart. It knows everything.
-Paulo Coelho, author (1947-)

Melli is the only dog whom I have treated and who has had a cancerous growth. I have not treated other cancer cases. When starting the treatment, there was not much hope for a successful result.

Melli was a 7-year-old Spanish water dog, in whose left rear leg an abnormal formation had appeared: a lump with a diameter of almost one inch. The lump was located on the outer edge of her left rear leg, next to the leg's lowest joint. The vet had taken thin needle samples of the lump, which had been identified as a malignant sarcoma. The vet had recommended an operation of the lump and of the left knee's lymph gland.

107

About two weeks later, on the operation day, the vet examined the lump and reported that the growth had fastened itself to the leg's periosteum. In this short space of time, the growth had turned firmer and its boundaries had become less precise. Also, the gland was now considerably harder. According to the vet, the findings also suggested that the tumor was of a quickly spreading type. The treatment would be an amputation of the entire limb, as a mere operation of the formation attached to the bone would not suffice. Melli's owners decided that such a radical measure would be too much. They could not think of Melli's leg being amputated and were prepared to try out my treatment: at least it would do no harm. Once the operation was abandoned, during my treatment Melli did not receive other medication than the thyroid medicine that she had been on since she was small.

On my first visit, Melli was a little shy; she growled and tried to run away. Apparently this was normal, Melli did not like visitors at all, contrary to the family's other dog, Melli's "little sister" Halla. Halla would have been an easy one to treat. Quicker than usual, however, Melli let herself be petted and even have her sore leg be slightly probed, while her owner was holding her. We chose a chair for the treatment, which then turned into our regular treatment place. Melli would jump onto the chair in front of the window and sit with her plastic toy chicken in her mouth, and I would draw a chair next to her. At first I petted Melli and told her that I am only probing the leg and trying to help. Melli looked with her wise eyes from under her brows and fringe. I had prepared myself for Melli's treatment by meditating and by giving myself an energy treatment, in the same way that I usually prepared myself for a treatment. Part of the preparation was also that while driving, I practiced Bengston's method, meaning that in my mind, I went through images of what I myself wanted to happen. One of the images that came to me was an image of Melli on a summer's day, as we were celebrating Melli's recovery. This image was now the goal, toward which the treatment would be leading us. When I was about to start the treatment, I said in my mind: "I am channeling the highest possible energy to Melli, which Melli is ready to receive. Everything will happen in the best possible way, just as is intended." With this sentence, I had learned to step aside in order to make way for the treatment and to act as a mere channel for the therapy.

The first treatment was mostly about getting to know each other, and I wanted to get a general picture of Melli. The dog's left rear leg felt much warmer than the rest of her body. I also treated her head, but only a little: the dog did not like it when I put my hands on her earlobes. When treating people, on the first visits, I sometimes treat the area of the head for as much as half of the treatment time, but in the case of Melli, I had to start increasingly trusting my own inner feeling. So I mainly treated her leg, and also a little her head and chest. During follow-up visits, I often proceeded so that I started with the head area, petted the dog and felt if I could sense heat or a need to treat a specific area. Then I would mostly proceed by giving the treatment with one hand on the dog's chest and another on her leg, on top of the lump, or by placing both hands on each side of the sick leg. Usually I would try out all four legs, to see if I could feel heat or differences between them. Especially at the beginning, there was a big difference between the left rear leg and the other three legs. The difference with the other rear leg was not as substantial as with the front legs. While healing, I would let my thoughts run freely. However, often my head would empty in the course of the treatment.

109

When I was treating Melli, her owner or another family member would join us, and our talking would ensure that I would not overly concentrate on "healing." I treated each spot just as long as it felt necessary, and usually the entire treatment would last about 30 minutes. The second treatment was the longest as I treated Melli for over an hour. At first, Melli was fairly easy to treat, but toward the end of the treatment, she started moving in a way that suggested that it was getting to be enough. After each session Melli received a treat as a reward for being such a good patient.

We decided with Melli's owners that to begin with, I would give Melli an intensive course of energy treatments. I would treat Melli two or three times a week to see how the treatment would start to have an effect. In addition to the local treatment, especially at the beginning of the treatment, I would also give daily remote care, sometimes even twice a day. At first I treated only Melli, then I added her to my remote care list, and gave joint care to the people and animals on my list. While giving remote care, I noticed how clearly I could bring back to mind the feeling of treating Melli on location. In my hands, I could feel Melli's fur: it was curly, soft and at times moist when Melli had just come in from a walk outside. I could also sense the smell of the fur and the way it looked. In my mind, I sent the treatment first to the area of the head, then to the neck, the stomach, and the back and legs. I felt in my mind where treatment was needed, what caught my attention or was radiating heat. Sometimes it even felt that the connection was better than when sitting on location, as from a distance, I had the space to listen to my own sensations.

The treatments that took place in the first month felt especially meaningful. When giving local care, I felt that the area of the lump pulled energy toward itself, often so that the area would radiate heat, signaling that this was the very place that needed healing. Usually the heat could be felt very strongly at the start of the treatment, and then it would subside. Also the chest and the area of the thyroid gland seemed to crave for healing, in other words I had the feeling that I should put my hands on those areas that reflected heat. Naturally, I would always treat the sick leg, but also the chest and the head, and, in addition, I would scan through the dog's body: were there hotter places somewhere and did I get an intuitive feeling as to where else treatment was needed? At times I would treat the stomach, sometimes an eye and other places that felt acute. Often in such situations Melli's owner would report that Melli had had stomach aches, or that the dog had hurt herself on a walk in the forest or something of the sort, which would support my own sensations. Increasingly, I started recognizing the ailments that had developed over time and even the type of the painful area, whether it was a sprain, a wound or something else.

The individual treatments followed a similar pattern: the dogs always ran to greet me when I arrived to give the treatment – Halla, excited, prepared to jump against me, and Melli looking from under her brows and fringe, even growling at me. The owner would order Melli to go sit in her treatment chair by the window, and Melli would obey and jump, often with her favorite soft toy in her mouth. The toy would often stay in her mouth for the entire duration of the treatment. Mostly, after I had treated Melli's leg for a while, she was ready to leave. Often at that point, I would also feel that the treatment sufficed, but I would continue treating for a little while yet if it was possible to keep Melli still. The dog

111

would certainly get hot; I often felt really hot, too. The other one of the dogs, Halla, would have liked to be treated, too, and time allowing, I would treat her as well. Many times, after treating Melli I would treat the rest of the family, depending on which acute ailments they had, and usually there were plenty of them in this active family.

The first month was the most intensive time of the treatment, and it also made me grow as an energy healer. At first it felt difficult to go treat a patient who was so sick. At the same time, I had a strong feeling that I knew what I was doing. I can only do my best. At any rate, I am not the one doing the healing, but am only acting as a channel, and mediating energy. I can only transmit love and visualize a good and perfect end result in my mind. Everything will happen just as it is meant to, in the best way possible. Even if it so happened that Melli didn't make it, I would still have been there to help her in the transition, and to support Melli's family. One day about three weeks into the treatment was particularly difficult; then I cried for Melli and felt powerless. I cried simultaneously for all my own losses. It felt as if two parts inside of me were talking: one was crying and the other was consoling and offering support. Eventually, the latter said to let go of everything. "How am I important in this process? All I am doing is mediating energy and love, and I can only hope for the best and visualize a good ending for the story." It was as if something had rolled out of the way, and I understood my role as part of the whole. After that day I had no problems treating, and the treatments seemed to have gained something. My hands also seemed to warm up faster at the start of a treatment.

My actual sensations during the treatments would vary a lot. The treatments started going faster each time, and it felt that I was "increasingly tuned to the same frequency with the dog." It became easier to prepare myself for the treatment and it did not seem to take as long to get it started. I would meditate or give myself an energy treatment before each session with Melli, and in my mind, I would contact – so I thought – our joint energy field, or our joint knowledge. In the course of Melli's treatment as well as others, the sensation has grown that we all have access to shared information. None of us are separate individuals, completely apart from others, but a part of a shared, joint knowledge. What I felt the strongest during the treatments was heat. A heat that was different, sharper than when I just caught the dog by its paw and held the paw in my hand. The feeling was stronger, a feeling that one should not let go now, but stay with it and mediate energy.

I decided that I would not take the size of the lump as a measure of the treatment's success, but rather that I would follow Melli's well-being. Naturally, I would check the size of the lump at least to begin with each time, but I tried not to let the lump's development influence me. After the first one and a half months, I even started getting the feeling that the treatment was beginning to suffice. There did not seem to be such a great need for the treatment anymore. The situation was slightly undermined by the fact that the lump was still intact; at times it seemed to have even grown a little, and at others, diminished. However, since the dog felt good, or even better, there did not seem to be a cause for concern. Sometimes, on the evening of the treatment day, the dog would be in such a wild and happy mood that it would run and jump around like a puppy, according to the owner. The treatments went on

113

and the lump seemed to begin to shrink in size. It shrunk really slowly, but it did shrink, or at least it didn't grow. Melli was still well and played with Halla as when she was a puppy. I kept treating her, although there didn't seem to be such a need for it anymore. After less than half a year from the start of the treatments, we found that Melli's lump had disappeared! The leg hadn't emitted a similar heat as in the early weeks for ages! Instead, I was now treating Melli's right eye, which seemed to warm up a little and emit a slight discharge. Perhaps Melli had hurt it against a branch while running in the forest or elsewhere.

Once, a couple of months later, when I went to treat Melli, the left leg was sore again. When I heard that the same leg was ill again, I feared the worst, and felt a little tense when I went to see the dog. However, the feeling changed quickly: the area of the lump didn't feel warm. There was no lump to be felt, and the sensation was more that of a rupture of a muscle in the leg. The leg's thigh muscle seemed to warm up, but it felt nothing like before. I proceeded with the treatment as before, and after about half an hour, the treatment seemed complete and the dog ran to the kitchen to fetch her reward. Later on, I found out that the leg had healed within about a week, so it may well have been a rupture as I had suspected.

Altogether, Melli received over 10 hours of local treatment and, in addition, at least the same amount of remote healing for her leg. The most active phase of the treatment lasted about 3 months. In addition to the lump healing, Melli lost weight during the treatment. The lump in the leg didn't recur. Now, at the time of writing this, Melli is well and 10 years' old. After the treatment, Melli's thyroid medication was also reduced.

Soon after the lump had disappeared, Melli was taken back to see the vet. Recovery without an operation was not supposed to be possible. Melli received a clean bill of health. The vet's comment upon Melli's surprise recovery was: "Let's be grateful for this!"

On Melli's treatment process

The attached table features observations on Melli's treatment process and on the changes in her lump, as well as my own thoughts and feelings during the treatments.

Ever since I learned Reiki, I have thought that it isn't something that can be turned on and off, but instead it follows me in all my actions. Especially in the early stages, I would draw the Reiki symbols on my hands, and visualize them in my mind at the start of the treatments. I would also go over the litany "I am now sending the highest possible energy that the healee is able to receive, everything happens in the best possible way and the healee receives help immediately". I used all of this while treating Melli, too. I prepared myself beforehand for every treatment, and went over things to have them clear in my mind. I can't manipulate or guide the energy independently, as it goes where the healee is ready to receive it. I gave energy healing following my intuition. I listened constantly to my own feelings and gave the treatment in the best way I could. At times, I used Bengston's method and at others, I intensified the treatment with Reiki symbols. What was interesting was that many family members had ailments on the left side, just like Melli.

Number of treatments	Day from the start	Duration	Size of the lump	Own thoughts and feelings
1	-	0:30	Lump about one inch, attached to the bone, hard, quite firm and round	The whole left leg warm, right leg not. I also treated the chest; feeling of needing treatment. I heard afterwards that the dog also suffered from thyroid gland insufficiency, for which medication. Melli was slightly on guard while being treated. Great that she could stay still and be treated this well!
2	3	1:15	Lump 1 inch, on left rear leg	Heat could be felt at the start of the treatment around the lump for ca. 5 min, a warm area also around the left rear knee and the chest. The thyroid gland feels as if it is repelling. A cheerful patient.
3	6	0:40	Lump intact, hard, maybe the lower part is softer?	The leg felt warm at first, but the feeling stopped and there was no longer a difference to be felt between the two sides. The chest attracted energy; the thyroid gland could not be felt.
4	10	0:30	Intact	The leg gets warmer, the same feeling as before.
5	14	0:30	The lump feels the same as before	Feeling of heat and burning around the lump for ca. 5 min. Passed. Elsewhere no feeling of a need for treatment.
6	19	0:40	Lump intact, ca. 1 inch long, could have spread a little, not significantly.	At first, it seemed as if the leg was a little sore while walking, but the dog did run. Was in her element, ate well and played etc. I treated the leg, with my other hand alternately on the opposite side of the leg and under the thyroid gland. Warmed up, especially around the lump. Also the chest seemed to require treatment.

Number of treatments	Day from the start	Duration	Size of the lump	Own thoughts and feelings
7	28	0:40	Lump little less than 1 inch, slightly smaller (!), attached to the bone	Warmth and tingling in the palm while treating. The area of the thyroid gland also needed treatment, as did the stomach. No feeling of a need to treat all the time, rather the feeling that angels were waving and saying: "We will take care of this". :) Note: Interesting feeling, as angels are not mentioned in Reiki or in Bengston's method.
8	34	0:30	Lump intact, maybe slightly smaller	During the first 5 min, a feeling of warmth around the lump, but it receded. My own thoughts before the treatment: letting go, trusting that things will work out. Support from my own, Melli's and all healing angels. Together we can do this.
9	42	0:30	Lump intact.	Feeling of warmth and tingling, difficult to say where things are at... No need to, I am just giving treatment. Thoughts before the treatment: I need to surrender and let things happen. I am just doing my best.
10	49	0:30	Lump smaller...	No more aches in the thigh. Interesting. Feeling that it is not necessary to treat so much.
11	59	0:30	Lump slightly smaller, maybe smaller than ever before?	Melli was slightly reluctant to come to the treatment, as before, but stayed. No warmth to be felt around the leg or elsewhere either that much, perhaps a good sign? Maybe treatment is not needed so much? Dream at night: I was hiding with Melli in some basement; someone searched with a flashlight and found us. Melli ran in the dream!

Number of treatments	Day from the start	Duration	Size of the lump	Own thoughts and feelings
12	74	0:40	Lump the same as before	A slight feeling of warmth, but not so much. Sense of undulating and flow, but nothing else, really. Feeling of warmth around the stomach. I treated the leg, the other hind leg, the hip, the stomach, and the eye. In the white of the left eye, there was a small lump (could it have been just a cut).
13	81	0:40	The lump of the leg intact	More heat could be felt than before. There has been a lump in Melli's eye for the past three weeks. Feeling of warmth, but not that much.
14	89	0:30	The lump of the leg is intact	Lump in the eye has maybe grown a little. The eye is also running. Feeling of warmth, but not that much. Melli doesn't want to be treated for very long. The reason could partly well be that in the treatment, it gets very hot, also for the healer. Personally I can't feel the heat as before. Usually I hold one hand over the chest and the other over the lump. Also, I have treated the whole hip, the stomach, and now also the eye. The eye doesn't feel quite the same as the leg's lump, but could it be part of the same ailment...
15	142	0:20	-	The area of the lump doesn't feel as hot, it has spread evenly around the leg. It feels quite good.
16	144	0:20	The lump is smaller	It felt good, the leg feels healthy, the lump has decreased!
17	179	0:30	Gone!	The lump in Melli's leg has disappeared! There is no feeling of warmth at all on the leg, where the lump used to be! The right eye seemed to warm up and festered a little. The stomach seemed to warm up a little, too, as did the chest and the area around the thyroid gland.

Number of treatments	Day from the start	Duration	Size of the lump	Own thoughts and feelings
18	257	0:30		Melli's left leg has been sore. The place of the lump didn't feel warm, but rather like a torn muscle. Some areas warmed up, but not that much. (Later addition: the leg was in good condition within about a week, so it may well have been a sprain).
Total	257 days	10:15		
	actively ca. 3 months			

CHAPTER 8. Regarding experiences

The only source of knowledge is experience.
- Albert Einstein (1879-1955)

What, then, do my own and my clients' observations tell about energy healing, in addition to helping them relax?

The healer has a feeling of heat in the hands. Some places feel warmer than others. The healee also has a sense of heat. The body always emits heat, which is due to energy transfer from warmer materials to cooler ones. What is experienced in a treatment cannot, however, be explained by the transfer of heat alone. I often feel heat, as do my clients, even though my hands are cold. The feeling of heat also changes while treating. At times it even feels like the heat is flowing into my hands. And at other times, there is a strong feeling of heat in some other part of the body, which then suddenly stops. I also wonder why I feel that heat emanates differently from different injuries. Sometimes I can even tell which part of the body requires treatment based on the sense of heat alone.

The sense of heat is also a recurrent observation about treatments among my clients. Often the heat and relaxation alone seem to help unravel the body's aches and tensions. There are exceptions, too, to the sense of heat. A few times, instead of heat, both my clients and I have experienced the treatment as being cold. Instead of heat, I would feel a cold stream in my hands, although otherwise the temperature of the hands would be normal. Sometimes the cold is explained as a deficit in life energy or a blockage in the energy body related to emotions. My personal feeling is that what matters is the temperature difference that I feel, whether it is cold or hot. During the treatment the temperature differences usually even out. You can find out more about my preliminary research, and attempts to understand heat, in chapter 10.

As an interesting note, I discovered similarities between my own sensations and the observations made by Nummenmaa et al. in their article "Bodily maps of emotions". For instance, if my client is experiencing deep sorrow in their life, the head and chest will feel particularly hot, and the area of the stomach will be hot as well.

Different types of ailments feel differently in the hands. In addition to the healee's body heat, different types of ailments, such as wounds, can also feel different. "Feeling" here refers both to the feeling in my hands and to my own intuition. It is difficult to say which has a more prominent role. Differences cannot always be felt. I discovered that I am better at sensing, if I don't expect any sensations, or when I have already given a few treatments to my healee. The number of sensations seems to correlate with the quality of the connection.

The healees' ailments are felt in the healer's own body. The healee thinks about the same things as the healer. One explanation for the sensations could be the mirror neuron system. Mirror neurons, sometimes referred to as empathy neurons, were discovered in the 1980s. They are nerve cells, whose task is to imitate, for instance, what another person does, feels and experiences. Thanks to the mirror

121

neurons, we can sense what another person feels when we touch them. The brain activation in reaction to touch, for instance, has been studied with magnetic resonance imaging. What the studies show is that the same brain areas are activated by both the person who is doing the touching and by the person who is touched. This has led to the conclusion that we don't just imagine that we experience the same feelings as others, but that we can actually feel the same feelings. The existence and purpose of mirror neurons has been the subject of many speculations on whether the mirror neurons are in fact related to observing and the coupling of events. The mirror neurons may be an explanation for our apparent ability to know each other's feelings and thoughts. Mirror neurons are a materialistic explanation for this phenomenon. I also became interested in reading about telepathy, which is communication through thoughts. Interesting research is being carried out on telepathy, such as the studies on telepathy demonstrated by autistic children by Dr. Diane Hennacy Powell. Powell studies autistic children, who often have challenges in social interaction and whose interest is often not naturally directed toward other people. Hence one would not expect such children to be able to read other people's thoughts. Diane Powell's studies indicate strongly that at least a part of the children are.

A healer receives or visualizes images, events and words, which the healee recognizes as having actually taken place. At first I considered these experiences to be a coincidence, but the longer I gave treatments, the more often the experiences occurred. It would seem like the clair senses, or spiritual capacities to sense, would be strengthened through giving treatments. It is as if energy healing would open a connection to a shared information.

The healer sees colors behind closed eyes; the healee also sees colors. My clients often see the same colors and movement as I. For me, the colors are a sign that the connection is formed in the treatment. In his article, Hayano writes about the Reiki teacher Barbara Matsuura and her sensations during treatments and Reiki activations. With closed eyes, Matsuura perceives the movement of the colors, and their transition from violet with a background of black, to violet with green in the center. At times, the colors can get really bright. The description corresponded with my own experiences during treatments. Barbara Matsuura considers color to be a sign of a perfect, pure, divine connection. Violet is also known to have the highest frequency and thus the highest vibration among the visible colors of the light spectrum.

There is a sense of connection to an external source of healing. Bengston, too, had similar experiences. It is important to transfer the "responsibility" over the success of the treatment somewhere to the exterior, beyond one's subjective self, so that the treatment doesn't stem from the ego. On the other hand, while giving treatments, I feel that I don't do it consciously, but rather that I am part of a whole. I am not significant, just a channel for the healing.

The treatment happens in a state of timelessness, with a feeling of moving to another space and a feeling of losing one's own boundaries. The state of consciousness changes while giving treatments. The state could be described as relaxation akin to meditation or hypnosis, in which the state is also focused. It is a feeling of not being separate, but rather a part of the unity of all things.

There is a feeling of flow in the body or of being in an "energy shower" while giving treatments. At first, I partly explained this to myself with suggestion, as you learn the idea of the flow of energy in the body when studying energy healing. The feeling varies between flow and the sense of being in an "energy shower." To my surprise, my clients described similar feelings of flow or vibration in the body, without knowing anything about energy healing.

Describing Melli's case objectively. In Melli's case, the result of the treatment was different than originally expected, or at least it was different from what the vet thought would happen. Of course, Melli's was an individual case, and you cannot draw conclusions from one case. However, what makes the case interesting is that at least with animals, you cannot say that suggestion for healing could take place in the same way as with humans. In Melli's case, you cannot suggest that Melli herself believed in the effect of the treatment and was therefore healed, like the placebo effect is often described. Therefore I consider the case to be even more important than when treating humans. At the very least, the issue should be studied further. The treatment should be repeated in the same way. Melli's case is indeed interesting and thought provoking. When the doctor no longer gives hope and already says goodbye to the patient, maybe there still is hope? Perhaps, when all other treatments have been stopped, one could still give energy healing, which at the very least will relax and can, for instance, relieve pain, and possibly even lead to healing?

When listening to my students' experiences, I have noticed that at some point while giving treatments, many energy healers will come across their own, special and meaningful healing experience that changes their relationship to healing. The experiences are often associated with an insight, on the level of the mind, of the healer being just a mediator. A student of mine treated her friend who was suffering from migraine. She began the treatment from the head area and felt heat just like her friend. When she moved her hands over the friend's shoulders, both felt as if an electric shock had passed through the friend. Both were frightened and wondered what had happened. Otherwise, the treatment went on as usual, but the friend's migraine disappeared and it hasn't renewed since. Another one of my students treated her sister, who had suffered from IBD, an inflammatory bowel disease, since childhood. The sister had just been to a doctor's check-up and the situation was found to be still unchanged, and perhaps to have even spread to a larger area since the previous visit. My student gave energy healing to her sister. At least the healing wouldn't do any harm, and perhaps the energy treatment would help ease the stomach pains. After the next scan, the sister called and reported that there was no trace of illness anymore. The doctors were astonished by what had happened and the sister told them that she had received Reiki healing. The third energy healer treated her relative, who had breast cancer and who was heading for an operation. The breast had been scanned, showing a tumor. The relative was afraid that the breast would need to be completely removed. On the day of the operation, the relative called to say that no operation had been carried out after all. The tumor had disappeared. All these experiences confirmed the healers' call to listen to the heart and to do what they felt was their mission. All of them are now combining energy healing with other treatment forms that they are providing.

CHAPTER 9. Adjusting one's world view

"Reality is merely an illusion, albeit a very persistent one."
- Albert Einstein

The more I do energy healing, the more I encounter phenomena that do not fit my acquired model of the world. What should I do? I can try to adjust my experiences to fit the old model or look for a new model that would explain the phenomena. Or perhaps my own observations do not tell all?

About observations

We shape our worldview through our observations. Observations are also necessary for science, as the observations regarding phenomena form the foundation of all knowledge. All observations are studied objectively through scientific procedures, with the aim of being understood. Research attempts to find answers to questions, explain phenomena and combine the phenomena with prevalent theories.

Observations are also a dilemma for science. On the one hand, our experiences and observations provide material and data that tell us about a given phenomenon. On the other hand, science seeks objective truth that is independent of the observer.

What could one trust more than the knowledge gained through one's own observations? Understanding subjective, or first-hand experience has been one of the foremost challenges for science and philosophy throughout centuries. The philosopher Maurice Merleau-Ponty maintained in the 1940s that we must break our accustomed ways of viewing the world in order to really see it. He rejected the view that mind and body are separate. Merleau-Ponty would study, among others, anomalous experiences of his time, such as the phantom limb sensation, where a person feels his or her amputated leg. He stated that a human being is not like a machine. Merleau-Ponty held the opinion that it is not possible to describe an experience exhaustively based only on human physiology, even if all the possible information would be available. What we also need is to understand the mind.

Considering mind and body as separate as opposed to as a single entity stems from the early modern period in the 17th century, which can also be considered to mark the beginning of modern science. That is when science and religion became separated from each other. This was an important division for scientific development: the church would no longer dictate or control the direction of research with its own interpretations to the extent that it had before. Up until then, science had always been interpreted in the light of religion, which would restrain scientific advancement. As a matter of fact, many scientists of the time were also priests. As a result of the separation, the physical, material world was left for science to deal with, whereas the mental, spiritual side was left to religion. This was of considerable help for scientific development.

René Descartes, who also lived at the beginning of the 17th century, claimed: "We must study what kind of knowledge the human reason is capable of attaining before we engage in gathering information about individual objects." We must understand the mind and our own experience before we are able to assess what our observations actually tell us. The same also pertains to the interpretation of the results gained with measurement devices. In science, one speaks of the influence of the observer, in other words of how the act of observing, i.e., measuring, changes the observed phenomenon. When a thermometer is placed in a water bowl to measure the temperature, you are no longer measuring the same system as without the measurement device, as the thermometer is now included, with its own temperature. Often, there is an attempt to improve the quality of the observation with better measuring devices. The role of the observer is one of the most essential questions in quantum physics.

The observer is, therefore, of consequence, as the observer always influences the final result. Even if science would aim to find a reality independent of observations, there would be no sure proof of the actual existence of such a reality. After all, observations always form the starting point for empirical science.

Some scientific concepts

During my life, I have often encountered challenges with concepts when different worlds and views have met. In the world of science alone, various disciplines can differ considerably in their views. As I will be writing more about science and research in the following chapters, I will first seek to clarify some scientific and research terminology.

The aim of science is both to explain natural phenomena and to put these to use. Explaining refers to the description of phenomena with increasingly more detailed concepts and terminology while trying to formulate causal theories of phenomena that apply as generally as possible. First, there is the observation of the phenomenon. The phenomenon will be described as comprehensively as possible. The occurring changes, the phenomenon's characteristics, as well as the factors and the environment affecting it, will be identified. Science will seek to classify the phenomenon. Science and research are pursued through scientific methods, which may differ considerably between disciplines. *A scientific method* is a systematic way by which new knowledge is acquired, or old knowledge is further specified. The methods are objective ways to find a solution to the studied problem. You seek to measure and describe the phenomenon with qualifiers that relate to the observed characteristics. The measurement provides objective information on the phenomenon. Variables within the phenomenon itself are sought out, as well as the quantities that describe the phenomenon's environment and the characteristics upon which the phenomenon depends on. These will allow to describe the phenomenon precisely and systematically and observe its interfaces e.g., when the phenomenon occurs and are there any regularities. The need is to identify laws pertaining to the phenomenon. This information can be used to build prognoses in the circumstances similar to those in the research. When studying different phenomena, one can build a *model* of the investigated problem, which will describe the studied phenomenon from one viewpoint. *A hypothesis* is, on the other hand, a proposed explanation for a phenomenon that will be specified in more detail when further measurements will be taken, or additional data will be gathered on the phenomenon. A phenomenon can be explained and understood through an underlying *theory.* A theory often describes the behavior of several phenomena. Science relies on observations and replicable experiments. Thus, theories are experimental, empirical and thereby always open for reappraisal, should new material emerge. Even the most fundamental theories can prove imperfect. When increasing amounts of observations and experimental studies occur that science cannot explain, science itself will require change or clarification. Science has encountered such upheavals irregularly on a regular basis. One such upheaval started in physics at the beginning of the 20th century, along with the development of quantum mechanics and the theory of relativity, when it was no longer possible to describe all the observed phenomena with the Newton's model of classical physics.

The aim of science is to tell definite truths about the surrounding world. One of the most essential components of research is documentation. The progress of the research, the findings and measures taken must be documented precisely, so that they can be replicated when needed. A scientific article is often written of the research findings, and it is published, mostly in a peer-reviewed scientific publication. In a peer review, external experts or referees go over the material to be published. They will assess, among others, the factual content and scientific significance of the article and ask for clarifications, if necessary, before the article can be accepted for publication. With the peer review process, the scientific credibility of the research articles to be published is tested. Science is created piece by piece through such studies; together they form a whole.

The observed phenomena can thus be either linked to existing theories, or they can be phenomena that have not been observed before. New, unexplainable phenomena can teach us a lot and move research forward. Throughout time, people have encountered phenomena that they have not been able to explain. Phenomena, the explanation of which has required the creation of new models and which have shaped the worldview and scientific thinking of the time.

Often the changes in thinking have not happened easily. The priest, mathematician and astronomer Nicolaus Copernicus published as early as in 1530 his work of the heliocentric, sun-centered model of the solar system. The Church considered the Earth to be center of everything, and the thought that, instead, it is the Earth that orbits the Sun was revolutionary. The Church finally banned the theory. The physicist, philosopher and astronomer Galileo Galilei endorsed the Copernican thoughts. The Catholic Church considered the theories dangerous and heretical, and Galilei had to face Inquisition, which finally condemned him to house arrest for the remainder of his life for failing to bend to the Church's opinion.

Even many invisible and presumably imaginary things have proved to be real. As an example, one can mention the discovery of bacteria. At the beginning of the 19th century, it was common in Central Europe for almost every tenth mother to die in hospital due to puerperal fever. The hospital doctor Ignaz Semmelweis studied the situation and concluded that the students' dirty hands spread the illness to the patients. When hands started being washed, the death rate decreased. Nothing was known about bacteria at the time, and doctors thought that Semmelweis' conclusions were lacking in scientific foundation. He was laughed out of scientific circles. Semmelweis took this hard and died later in a mental asylum. It was only close to a hundred years later, at the end of the 19th century, when Louis Pasteur demonstrated the existence of bacteria and Joseph Lister invented how to disinfect wounds, that it was understood what Semmelweis had talked about, and he gained due recognition.

An analogy can be seen between Semmelweis' story and today. Many representatives of conventional medicine will dismiss homeopathy, for instance, although studies have already demonstrated that water seems to have many interesting characteristics, possibly akin to memory. More about these studies will follow in the subchapter of Chapter 12, entitled Mind and Matter.

Stories akin to those experienced by Galilei and Semmelweis can be found throughout the ages. When you have learned a particular way to view the world, you don't change it lightly. Even in everyday life, you can easily keep living according to the same formula, and you don't question things until the customary model is so broken that it forces you to reconsider other possibilities. Usually, the breaking of deeply held beliefs or models broadens one's perspectives, and the newly synthesized expanded view is often more truthful than the belief one started with.

You can broaden your own perspective with energy healing, for instance. The more I give energy treatments, the stronger I feel that the two different "worlds", the material and the energetic, that I inhabit are not contradictory. They are two sides of the same entity, and the sides just need to be combined.

WHAT IS THE "ENERGY" TRANSMITTED IN ENERGY HEALING?

Chapter 10. The energy of energy healing

"There is a force in the universe
which, if we permit it,
will flow through us and produce miraculous results."
- Mahatma Gandhi (1869-1948)

The word 'energy' used in spoken language rarely means the same thing as the term 'energy' in physics. Energy in spoken language often refers to energy at the level of the mind: the ability to act and being capable. In the context of energy healing, one speaks of energy that is channeled through the hands. What exactly does one mean by transmitting universal life energy? How is energy defined in physics? How does universal life energy differ from the energy usually discussed in physics? What is the energy of energy healing?

Energy in physics

It is difficult to provide an exact definition of energy due to its different forms. At its simplest, energy is defined as the capacity of a force, an object or a system to perform work, move or produce an effect. Energy describes the potential for change, meaning that it is always present in interactions, when a force is affecting, an object is changing shape or place, or when a system is undergoing change. As a matter of fact, energy is a process, which has a beginning, an action and a result. The action can also repeat itself. The power will tell how fast the energy is consumed, or $E = Wt$, where W is power and t is time.

One of the foremost pioneers of the understanding of energy was Michael Faraday, who discovered the connection between electricity and magnetism at the beginning of the 19th century before the concept of energy had even been officially defined. It turned out that other forms of energy, such as kinetic energy, potential energy, heat and chemical energy, were all connected. The different forms of energy may also be converted from one form to another. However, the energy is a conserved quantity, meaning that the total energy of a system remains constant in energy transformations. In other words, energy can neither be created nor destroyed. This is described in the law of conservation of energy, which is also known as the work-energy principle. In other words, the total sum of energy that exists in the universe today is exactly the same as when the universe was born. All the energy of the universe thus stems from one and the same common source. Notice the surprising similarity with the concept of universal life energy, which is also thought to stem from the source.

Energy is also closely connected with the concept of field. Initially, it was Faraday who introduced the concept of field to physics. According to Faraday, two electrically charged bodies can influence each other from a distance, even when they are not in contact with each other. This could be understood as the bodies being in an energy field through which they interact. Again, notice the similarity with distant healing: two bodies can influence each other even from a distance through the field. At the time, there were attempts to describe the field with ether, for instance, which had been discussed ever since antiquity. Ether was not thought of as being tangible, physical matter, it was thought to be invisible and lacking mass, yet filling the whole universe. Back then, ether was generally discussed as having a spiritual nature. Even during the late 19th century, there were attempts to explain many phenomena in physics with ether, including light and electromagnetic phenomena. Later the concept of ether was gradually dropped, but the concept of the field remained.

With the advent of Einstein and his theory of relativity, the understanding of energy changed again: matter, too, or mass, contains energy, which can be freed from matter for instance in a nuclear reaction. Energy is not conserved, nor is mass, but they have a connection between them. This is described by Einstein's famous equation $E = mc^2$, where E is energy, m is mass and c is the speed of light. Special theory of relativity, which Albert Einstein published in 1905, is the current physics' dominant concept of space, time and electromagnetism. It applies only to inertial i.e., non-moving, coordinate systems with constant in constant velocity, as the theory cannot deal with accelerating, or decelerating movement. The general theory of relativity was created to deal with these cases, where two different coordinate systems accelerate from each other. The general theory of relativity differs from our usual way of thinking about time and describes how time and space are curved and how curving is a characteristic of gravity. Einstein wanted to create a Theory of Everything (TOE), which would combine all the theories, but the dream was to remain unfulfilled when Einstein died in 1955. The Theory of

Everything, which would bring all the models together, has been dreamt of for decades, but there is still no unified field theory. Many physicists, among them Stephen Hawking, have considered it possible that such a theory will never see the light. Generally, the strongest TOE candidate is thought to be the superstring theory.

Thus, in physics, energy can be described as a potential to make things happen in interactions. There can also be energy transfer between bodies or systems. For instance the energy of food transfers to the person when eating.

Universal life energy

Over 2500 years ago, Lao Tzu, the father of Taoism, described universal life energy as follows:

Look, it cannot be seen – it is beyond form
Listen, it cannot be heard – it is beyond sound
Grasp, it cannot be held – it is intangible
These three are indefinable, they are one

Universal life energy is discussed in many different cultures and it has many names. Freely translated and interpreted, it refers to "energy or power that exists everywhere in nature." In Japan, this is referred to with the term *ki*, which is also in the name of Reiki: the founder of Reiki Mikao Usui described the universal life energy by the name "*Reiki*". "*Rei*" means something miraculous, etheric, supernatural and sacred, even divine. "*Rei*" is the higher consciousness behind everything. It is what guides the entire universe and exists everywhere, in living as well as inanimate bodies. "*Ki*", on the other hand, refers to the energy of the universe. It is non-physical and is present everywhere: in living beings, organisms, humans, animals and plants. It is said that when there is a lot of *ki*, the person feels well, is strong, confident and enjoys life. When there is less *ki*, the person is weak and is more likely to get ill. *Ki* can be replenished with food, drink, the air that one breathes, the air and nature in the outdoors, and with sleep. One can also increase *ki* with physical exercises, breathing exercises, and, for instance, with meditation. When a person dies, *ki* leaves the physical body.

Ayurveda, the thousands of years old, ancient Indian medicine, discusses *prana*. *Prana* is described in many old texts and it is said to have initially meant breathing. *Prana* is said to be life energy, which controls the beating of the heart and breathing. It enters the body through breathing and goes into every cell in the body. Names used in other cultures to denote *ki* and *prana* are, for instance, *chi* or *qi* in China, *pneuma* in Greece and *mana* in Hawaii.

Like energy in spoken language, *universal life energy* can mean different things in different contexts. In the following, I will use the term *qi* to refer to universal life energy, as it is perhaps most commonly used in the West. Initially, *qi* meant air, steam, fog, breath, spirit or soul, from which it gradually expanded to denote energy in general. *Qi*, in other words, can be used to denote energy, in a way that is similar to how energy is often described also in Western physics. Nowadays, however, *qi* is more commonly used to refer to the part in *qi* that is "alive", that is life energy, which sets apart the living from the inanimate. It is also the energy that is referred to in the context of energy healing. *Qi* flows through everything that is alive and its balance is described with *yin* and *yang* (masculine and feminine, positive and negative). Associated to the flow of energy are the meridians of Chinese medicine, the channels of energy, and the chakras or the body's energy centers, derived from India.

Sometimes the Reiki healers speak of a particular *"Reiki energy"*, which is described as being more than *universal energy*, because it involves a positive guiding influence or intention, a direction. One cannot actually influence the direction of the treatment, that is, for instance, one cannot manipulate another person to behave in the way that one desires. One can just express a wish and then let go of it.

In ancient India, China, Japan and Egypt, the physical human body was thought of as being surrounded by energy fields. Around the body, there are several subtle energy bodies that universal life energy flows through and into the physical body. The fields interact between themselves, and also between different people and the environment. It is possible to perceive the fields with touch, and likewise, it is possible to affect the flow of universal energy in the fields.

In the context of the research on energy healing, one refers to the *subtle energy*, sometimes also *bioenergy*, which is the joint term for all the descriptions of universal life energy. Also added to the list are often love, the power of thought, consciousness, intention and intuition. The terms subtle energy and bioenergy are used to distinguish from the "real" energy of a physical model. Subtle means consisting of very small parts, which is well suited here, as we are dealing with a phenomenon that is often said to be so subtle as to be challenging to measure. There is no common, unambiguous view of subtle energy, and it is not included in the current "official" scientific model. There are studies that seek to measure it indirectly via its effects. The notion of it being measurable differs from traditional views on universal life energy, in which it is thought of as being metaphysical, and as such beyond physical measurements.

How to explain the energy of energy healing?

In physics, the term energy is used to explain the behavior of matter. In energy healing, what is dealt with is intangible, immaterial energy at the level of the mind. In other words, it is not the same kind of energy. It is true that in energy healing, too, one transfers information, which, in a sense, is also energy. Actually, instead of speaking of "channeling energy" in energy healing, we ought to speak of "information". Different viewpoints to energy are needed to better describe the whole, just as in quantum physics, describing the behavior of light requires both the wave and the particle models.

WHAT DOES SCIENCE SAY ABOUT ENERGY HEALING?

CHAPTER 11. Quantum physics – we are vibrating energy

"Everything we call real
is made of things
that cannot be regarded real".
- Niels Bohr, physicist (1885-1962)

Around the turn of the millennium, I was conducting research related to my Ph.D. on the subject of biodegradable plastics. A model as accurate as possible was required to describe the interactions, and for that, quantum physics was needed. I performed quantum mechanical calculations of the model molecules of biodegradable materials on supercomputers, and the model developed described the biodegradable plastics extremely well.

Once again, quantum physics could provide answers to my questions – related this time to energy healing. Could we say, on the basis of quantum physics, that energy healing works?

Opposites are complementary

Quantum physics is one of the most mystical fields in natural science. Of all the theories, it has advanced the development of technology the most by introducing many applications. In the book *Quantum Enigma* (2006), Bruce Rosenblum and Fred Kuttner estimate that the

141

applications of quantum theory such as computers, lasers, Blu-ray players, etc., count for as much as one third of the Unites States' current economy. In spite of the extensive applications of quantum theory, the field is very difficult to understand and it is even said that no one in the world fully comprehends quantum physics.

At the time of its birth, quantum physics contained revolutionary ideas, which set it apart from previous theories. Within the first thirty years of the 20th century, revolutionary changes occurred in the theories of physics, as well as in the philosophical questions and concepts of reality. Basically, quantum physics addresses ontological questions. In other words, it aims to provide answers to the question of the nature of reality. After the 17th century separation of science and church, a mutual rapprochement was now occurring again. A real understanding of science was seen as requiring philosophy, too. The changes brought by the discovery of quantum physics were so tremendous that even today, the significance of quantum physics is not fully grasped. In this chapter, I will attempt to describe the change brought on by quantum physics, and the revolutionary ideas that questioned the ability of the materialistic worldview alone to fully describe the world. Especially for a researcher, it is essential to keep an open mind concerning different, alternative ideas, as one's own view of reality affects the research. It is easy to leave evidence that one doesn't personally consider important or even possible as not worth paying attention to, such as: *"You see what you seek for, as what you seek for, you will find."* This goes for all of us: our personal views will easily lead us to look for answers in the same direction as where they have been found before, and as a consequence, something of significant importance may remain unnoticed.

The possible connection between quantum physics and oriental philosophies is often brought up, especially when talking about the more unusual traits of quantum physics. The two would indeed seem to have some kind of connection. It is said, for instance, that the researchers who have been most influential in the birth of quantum physics, such as Erwin Schrödinger and Albert Einstein, studied Vedanta in great detail while developing quantum physics. Vedanta is a Hindu philosophy based on sacred Indian Veda texts, which includes the notion of the divine origin of the spirit - the notion that everything is essentially one, and that different religions are of the same origin. The thinking of Schrödinger, for instance, is reflected in the following sentence drawn from an autobiography written in the summer of 1918:

"Nirvana is a state of pure, blissful knowledge (...). It has nothing to do with the individual. The ego or its separation is an illusion. Indeed in a certain sense, two "I's" are identical, namely when one disregards all special contents - their Karma. The goal of man is to preserve his Karma and to develop it further (...). When man dies, his Karma lives and creates for itself another carrier."

The connection between physics and Veda also interests many contemporary physicists. Among them, theoretical physicist Dr. John Hagelin has familiarized himself with Vedic knowledge and goes as far as to suggest that Veda equals the "Theory of Everything" combining all other theories, that is the Grand unified theory, or superstring theory.

143

According to him, the Vedic tradition is founded upon the complete knowledge and practical application of the ultimate reality, which in the modern scientific language is called the unified field. The view has not met with wider approval as of yet in the scientific community.

Quantum physics, which is also referred to as quantum mechanics, was developed in the 1920s to describe molecular and atomic level phenomena. The concept of atomic structure, of which matter is composed, is in itself much older: already in Greek philosophy, in 400 BC, Democritus, together with the philosopher Leucippus, presented the idea that matter was composed of undivided and unchanging parts that were surrounded by an empty space, making the movement of the parts possible. These parts were referred to by the name *atomos* or "indivisible", and this is also where the word "atom" stems from.

In physics, the atomic hypothesis became topical again only in the 19th century. At first, the hypothesis was only theoretical, without applications. However, it was taken into use in chemistry, especially on the basis of the chemist and physicist John Dalton's work. Dalton's research pointed to the atomic nature of matter. He developed the first atomic theory and published, among others, the first table of relative atomic weights. His initial list contained only 6 elements of periodic table. These atoms of different elements were able to combine in simple whole-number ratios to form chemical compounds.

Atomic physics made rapid progress at the beginning of the 20th century, when it was no longer possible to explain many phenomena on the basis of the classical model of physics developed by Isaac Newton in the 17th century. Newton's model is a set of laws, which describe the relationship between a body and the forces that act upon it, and the body's motion in response to those forces. The model is unable to describe, for instance, the blackbody radiation or the photoelectric effect.

In the year 1900, Max Planck proposed a hypothesis of the electromagnetic radiation occurring in discrete amounts of energy or quanta. The energy of a light quantum or photon could be presented in the form $E = hf$, with E standing for energy, h being a variable called Planck's constant and f the frequency of the radiation.

The central assumption behind his proposition was the supposition that electromagnetic energy could be emitted only in quantized form, i.e., discrete packets of energy. This approach described the experimentally observed blackbody spectrum well. Later on, however, it was experimentally proven that quantization of energy really does occur and that photons do appear in nature. Light transfers energy in the form of photons. The viewpoint was exceptional when compared to the previous theories. According to Planck's hypothesis, action on a subatomic level happens in discrete jumps and the energy was, thus, assumed having discrete values - meaning that it can only be transferred in individual "packets". In previous theories, energy was continuous, and could be transferred in any amount, allowing the use of continuous function mathematics in the analysis.

The discovery of the quantization of energy and ensuing interpretations led to the birth of quantum mechanics. Historians have held different views on whether Planck really understood how revolutionary his thoughts were and the kind of development that they would set in motion within physics. Due to the quantum hypothesis, many consider Planck as the father of quantum theory. Planck himself was modest and didn't seem to view his own role as particularly important, but emphasized instead the role of others. Planck received the Nobel Prize in Physics in 1918 for his discovery of the quantization of energy, and in his Nobel speech, he thanked other researchers who had also adopted the idea. In his speech, he mentioned especially Albert Einstein, who used the notion of quantum to explain many phenomena related to electromagnetic radiation, among them the photoelectric effect. The photoelectric effect refers to what happens when electrons are emitted from a material that has absorbed electromagnetic radiation. One inexplicable observation was that the maximum kinetic energy of the released electrons did not vary with the intensity of the light, as expected according to the classical, electromagnetic wave theory, but was proportional instead to its frequency. Einstein explained the phenomenon by way of light quanta: the light energy is carried in discrete quantized packets. Each particle of light, or photon, contains a fixed amount of energy, or quantum, that depends on the light's frequency. Einstein received the Nobel Prize for Physics, too, in 1921 for his research on the photoelectric effect.

According to Einstein's theory, light behaves dualistically. It has characteristics of both waves and particles: at times, light behaves like a wave and at others, like a particle. Light-particle dualism means that electromagnetic radiation, like light, has characteristics of both waves and particles. Young's double-slit experiment is one of the most famous

146

examples illustrating this duality. The experiment was originally performed as early as in 1802, and with it, Thomas Young demonstrated the wave-like character of light. However, in the course of the 19th century, the particle-like nature of light gained considerable support and it was only with the help of the light quantum hypothesis that it became possible to explain the phenomenon in more detail. Light can be either particles or waves, depending on how it is observed. As the physicist Richard Feynman puts it, the phenomenon is absolutely impossible to explain in any classical way. The double-slit experiment has in it the heart of quantum mechanics, and it contains the whole mystery.

In the double-slit experiment, the beam of photons or light particles is aimed at a wall with two holes, and through that to another wall. In the original experiment in the 19th century, the wall with two holes was lit by sunlight. A wave pattern is formed on the second wall, which is a sign of the wave-like character of light. As the wave passes though both slits, it essentially splits into two new waves, each spreading out from one of the slits. These two waves then interfere with each other, and at certain points, where a crest meets a trough, they will cancel each other out, and at others, where crest meets crest, they will reinforce each other. A stripy pattern, called an interference pattern, is formed on the wall with the strongest line in the center and several lines on both sides.

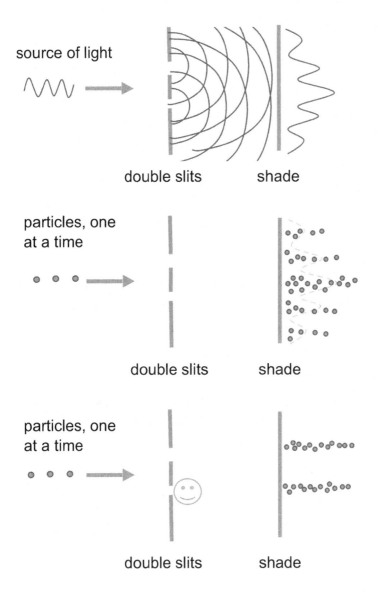

source of light

double slits   shade

particles, one at a time

double slits   shade

particles, one at a time

double slits   shade

Fig. Double slit experiment. In the image at the bottom of the page, 😊 depicts the location of the observer.

If the source of light is substituted with a light source firing light particles or photons separately one at a time, through the slits, the particles will hit the second wall one at a time, but together they will form a wave pattern, as if the particles knew where the other particles had hit. When one uses a particle detector to observe which slit each particle goes through, they, however, start behaving like particles. Only two lines are formed on the wall as an indication of particle-like behaviour. It is as if the particle knew that it was being watched. Light thus has a dual nature: sometimes it behaves like a particle and sometimes like a wave. Part of the particle-like nature is that the location of the particle is known at each moment. Part of the wave-like character is, in turn, that the location cannot be determined. The particle-like character and the wave-like character are contradictory, but both have to be accepted if one wants to understand all the characteristics of light.

The particle-like and wave-like natures are contradictory in the same way as yin and yang in Chinese philosophy. They are seemingly opposite, but mutually complementary forces. Two opposites can, in fact, be simultaneously complementary and interconnected. This duality can be seen in Chinese science, philosophy and medicine, which attempt to re-establish the balance of yin and yang through various means. In the symbol of yin and yang, a black and a white drop are intertwined. Yin is the black side with the white dot in it, and yang is the white side with the black dot in it. The symbol depicts how yin contains a seed of yang, and yang a seed of yin, and how they are continuously transforming, the one giving space to the other. Together, yin and yang represent perfect balance. The one could not exist without the other, for each contains the essence of the other and together they make up reality. If one of them is "true", it doesn't automatically mean that the other isn't true, unlike in mathematics, where the opposite of true is "false". As a sign of the connection between quantum mechanics and oriental philosophy, the Danish physicist Niels Bohr chose the yin and yang symbol, along with the text "Opposites are complementary" for his coat of arms when he was granted the Danish Order of the Elephant. However, Bohr, one of the foremost developers of quantum mechanics, held strictly onto a scientific approach and was unwilling to make any connecting interpretations in the direction of oriental philosophies. He aimed to keep science separate from mysticism.

The complementary nature of the atomistic world is a fundamental part of quantum mechanics. Two contradictory parts can complement each other and together they can form reality. No better, generally accepted explanation has been presented for the behavior of light and electromagnetic radiation. There are many similar, complementary quantities in quantum mechanics, such as, for instance, position and momentum, and energy and time. The more accurately we know one of the values, the less accurately we know the other. This is also known as the Heisenberg's uncertainty principle, which sets the limits for the measurement accuracy. It states that there are certain pairs of particles' properties that are impossible to determine simultaneously. When the measurement is performed, simultaneously one affects the value that is being measured, and it will no longer be the same as before measuring.

Do observations create reality?

In quantum physics, the observer has a very particular role.

In classical physics, an effect is preceded by a cause. The worldview is deterministic. Part of determinism is that in principle, everything is predetermined and all the physical phenomena are deterministic. Some physicists believe that all events can be traced back to the Big Bang. The course of events can be calculated mathematically when all the factors are known. This view doesn't take into consideration the effect of the mind. Classical physics is, however, based on a dualistic premise, in which the mental world always complements the physical world. The mind is always present, it can't be omitted, and thus the designer of the experiment isn't included as part of the physical determinism.

In quantum physics, the world is described with probabilities, which can be expressed through wave function. All possible alternatives or possibilities for different occurrences exist until that which will be realized is selected to happen. The selection occurs through observation. Observation can be a measurement performed by a measuring device, which outcome will eventually be observed by a human being, too. When, for instance, the result of the double-slit experiment is observed, the observation "collapses the wave function" giving a definite value to the measured quantity. Observing thus affects the observed reality. It can be said that when the observer makes a choice, all the other possibilities vanish and only one reality remains. Therefore, it can even be said that the observer "creates" his or her own reality and that the consciousness of the observer "collapses the wave function" to a certain state, that is to one of the options.

In quantum physics, therefore, things are not "real" until someone observes them. In contrast to the causality of classical physics, quantum mechanics doesn't tell anything about the reason why a certain reality becomes selected for realization. Quantum physics doesn't feature causal order in this respect, as opposed to classical Newton's physics. It is pointless to ask, where the particle was before. Quantum physics will not tell anything about direction, either; the direction of time has no importance. According to quantum physics, then, for instance in the case of observing the double-slit experiment, one can decide later, even after the experiment, whether the results are expressed in waves or particles, and they will vary accordingly. Thus, the observer not only affects the observation but is even considered to create the outcome.

Does consciousness, then, or the setup of the experiment, cause the wave function to collapse? There is no unanimous opinion on this among physicists. Radin et al., among others, have studied the effect of consciousness on the results of the double-slit experiment. The results of their research support the role of consciousness in the collapsing of the wave function. Research supports the notion that consciousness affects reality. Radin et al.'s research shows that the focus of the observer's attention has an effect on the spectrum formed on the second wall.

Later on, the Austrian physicist Erwin Schrödinger wanted to bring up the imperfections and the missing laws in quantum physics with a thought experiment known as Schrödinger's cat. According to quantum physics, all possible futures are in existence, and they all have a certain probability of occurrence. In the Schrödinger's cat thought experiment, there is a cat in a sealed container, along with equipment made up of a vial of poison gas and a radioactive substance that, with 50% probability, will decay within an hour. When it decays, it will release a particle that will activate the equipment and thereby open the poison vial, leading to the cat's death. Thus the cat is both alive and dead. When the box is opened and an observation takes place, one will either see a decayed nucleus and a dead cat, or an undecayed nucleus and a live cat. In the thought experiment, the question is asked: at which stage does the system cease to be a superposition or mixture of the two states, and becomes just one of them? Quantum physics doesn't have rules that would describe what happens and in which situations, and Schrödinger wanted to show that quantum physics isn't able to provide an answer to his question. Schrödinger was one of the foremost developers of quantum mechanics: Schrödinger's equation also carries his name, describing the particle's behavior in the same way as the classical mechanics' equation of motion describes the behavior of macroscopic particles. Schrödinger received the Nobel Prize for Physics in 1933 for developing the equation.

Many philosophical questions are associated with quantum mechanics and there are many interpretations, e.g., the Copenhagen interpretation, David Bohm's causal interpretation, and the many-worlds interpretation. The best known among these is the Copenhagen interpretation, which especially Niels Bohr and the German physicist Werner Heisenberg worked on. Heisenberg's aim was to create a clear, mathematical theory, whereas Bohr wanted to understand the thoughts and philosophical questions behind quantum mechanics. Wolfgang Pauli and Oskar Klein had an important role as the theory's editors and as mediators when the discussions came to an impasse. Bohr emphasized in his interpretations complementarity, whereas Heisenberg put an emphasis on the inaccuracy prevailing in the atomistic world. Einstein, too, disagreed with Bohr, but mostly over the concept of reality.

The Copenhagen interpretation contains the notion that there are different ways to describe and to see things. Science trusts observations, and we describe them in our everyday talk. Terms from classical physics can be of help here, as the concept of reality is similar. Classical physics maintains that the exterior world that we perceive can be observed in an objective manner. Problems arise only at the atomic level when the characteristics seem to vary according to the observer. There is no objective reality at the level of atoms. The act of measuring, and the observer, always influence the observation. One must apply the most suitable concept of reality to describe any given activity.

According to the Copenhagen interpretation, the waves are both "matter waves" and "probability waves": they contain all the information about a situation at the time of measurement. The question of the objectivity of observations and of "true" reality is indeed a more challenging one. At the level of atoms, the characteristics depend on the methods used in the measurements, or on what they have been observed with. For instance, in the wave-particle dualism, sometimes waves are observed, and sometimes particles. What, then, is the reality independent of observations? Is it even possible to find out such a thing?

Pauli claims that quantum physics ends up directing us toward the view that reality cannot be explained using the rational methods of the exact natural sciences. This, then, would mean that science, and quantum physics, lead to a concept of reality that includes a non-rational or irrational part. Science, religion and spirituality are indeed merging into one. If the irrational part cannot be described by scientific means, it would follow that it is no longer possible to completely and accurately describe observations with the methods used by the exact natural sciences. This is why the notion of the irrationality of reality has been mostly rejected, and the questions related to the concept of reality have been bypassed, too.

Einstein didn't agree with the concept of reality of the Copenhagen interpretation. He held a firm trust in the existence of an objective reality independent of observations. Also, Einstein didn't agree with quantum mechanics' statistical descriptions based on probabilities, and he considered quantum mechanics to be just a passing theory. Einstein's comment "God doesn't play dice with the world" reflects this attitude toward quantum mechanics. Bohr's answer to this was: "Einstein, don't tell God what to do." The argument between Einstein and Bohr went on for years. In 1935, together with his colleagues Boris Podolsky and Nathan Rosen, Einstein published the article: "Can

Quantum Mechanical Description of Physical Reality Be Considered Complete?". Bohr answered to this with an article by the same name in the same journal a few months later. The arguments didn't lead to a final solution to questions like the existence of an independent reality. However, they did suggest that there were features in nature that had to be accepted and that physics needed to adapt itself to. In a way, to believe in the existence of independent reality is a sign of faith, because it cannot be justified by scientific means.

Perhaps it can even be claimed that due to the differences between Bohr and Einstein, physics is still in a state of confusion. In a way, the Copenhagen interpretation was left unclear. As such it couldn't present, for instance, a unified view of reality. Many later interpretations of quantum mechanics, such as the many-worlds interpretation and David Bohm's causal interpretation, have adopted the still generally influential concept of the reality of classical physics. They hold many assumptions such as the validity of determinism and the existence of an objective reality that can be observed without affecting the measurement. The many-worlds interpretation assumes that reality is a completely objective entity, independent of the human being. Furthermore, it implies that all possible alternatives are realized in different worlds, but in such a way that they can never interact. Bohm's causal interpretation, in turn, makes the assumption of a hidden variable and explains how particles contain a structure whereby they can know beforehand, what kind of experiment will be performed on them. In other words, Bohm's model tells why quantum systems behave as they do and the results it gives are the same as in quantum mechanics. Thus, it is not possible to find out with experiments, whether Bohm's model is correct or not. Although both the many-worlds and Bohm's interpretation are often considered as realistic models of explanation, they have not met with general approval. There is not a single interpretation of quantum mechanics that is approved and agreed upon by the majority of physicists.

Is action at a distance possible?

In physics, action at a distance refers to non-local interaction, when particles separate from each other in space interact. A given particle can thus be influenced from a distance by changing its location or by affecting it otherwise without mechanical, physical contact. Initially, the term was used to describe gravitation and electro-magnetic interaction. In other words, non-local interaction is possible...

In quantum physics there are also other phenomena, in which one has an influence from a distance. With *entanglement*, also referred to as quantum entanglement, one describes how two or more quantum systems, or a couple or a group of particles, interact so that the quantum state of one affects the other. One cannot be described without the other. Thus, the state of one particle also contains information about the state of another particle. The particles can be considerably far apart, and yet they can be described as one entity. By changing one particle, one will affect the other one too. Both particles can therefore be described with a single, albeit spatially divided wave function. An entangled state or wave function can be born, for instance, when two particles collide or when a particle dissolves into new particles. The special feature of quantum mechanics is that according to the inaccuracy principle, measuring one particle will also alter the state of the other, entangled particle, and this change will occur immediately. At a speed faster than the speed of light, which ought not to be possible.

The possibility of such a particle moving faster than light has also been hypothetically suggested in physics. The first to speak of tachyons was the German physicist Arnold Sommerfeld at the beginning of the 20th century. Later, tachyons have been presented in the context of string theories, as well as in connection with the tunneling effect, among others. Tunneling is a phenomenon in quantum physics, where a particle can "tunnel" from one state to another, even though, according to classical physics, it should not have the energy to do so. Tachyons have, however, not attracted wide interest, because should they exist, they would break causality, the cause and effect relationship.

Einstein, naturally, did not accept the concept of entanglement, as it was opposed to the theory of relativity. Einstein referred to entanglement as *spooky action at a distance (Spukhafte Fernwirkung)*: the particles seem to interact, although an exchange of information between them ought not to be possible. Einstein suggested that quantum physics was lacking in this respect, and did not consider this possible. However, entanglement has also been proven experimentally many times, as well as the existence of non-local phenomena. Quantum entanglement happens all the time, and not just with atoms in laboratory circumstances. To generalize, one could say that entanglement is about how two separate particles, separate in space, can influence each other and still be one. That is, even if a space looks empty and the particles are seemingly separate, it is just an illusion.

Thus, we are, then, all one at some level. On the basis of these ideas, could it also be possible to find a model of explanation for remote healing?

We are vibrating energy

We still don't quite understand quantum physics or all that it entails. According to the materialistic view, everything stems from matter; it doesn't take consciousness nor the values or morale that guide our actions into account. Quantum physics requires change in the view of reality and acts as a bridge, reuniting the world of matter with the world of the spirit. And what may be even more significant: quantum mechanics has changed the notion of the kind of questions that can be asked in a meaningful way about nature's behavior within the domain of physics. Everything cannot be explained in detail, and similar assumptions don't apply as in classical deterministic physics. Knowing that one of two opposites is false doesn't mean that the other one is true, but rather they can be mutually complementary. Also, there is no objective truth, but everything depends on the observer!

Quantum physics has also introduced a new view on what we, humans, are: we are vibrating energy. Physics has been aware of this for only a little over a hundred years, and there is still a lot that we don't know or understand. According to quantum mechanics, then, matter is just an illusion. To quote Niels Bohr: *"Everything we call real, is made of things that cannot be regarded as real"*. Everything within and around us - the whole universe - is vibrating energy. Our body comprises of cells, which are made up of molecules, which in turn are made up of atoms. All matter is made up of atoms. These, on the other hand, are energy, and

159

the energy of the entire molecule, or atomistic system can be described with quantum mechanics. According to quantum mechanics, the energy and characteristics of all atomistic systems can be found out, in principle, by solving the wave equation $H\Psi = E\Psi$ of the atomistic system, called the Schrödinger equation, where H stands for Hamilton's operator, E for the system's energy and Ψ for the system's wave equation. The significance of Schrödinger's equation equals that of Newton's second law in classical mechanics; both describe movement. The equation looks simple, but it contains all the nuclei and electrons of the atomistic system and all possible different interactions between atoms, and in practice it becomes impossible to solve it accurately. So if one wants to solve the equation, it needs to be simplified, in other words, approximations are needed to describe both the energy and the state of the molecule. Therefore all computational and molecular modeling methods offer only rough approximations of the real situation.

Atoms are energy. They vibrate, spin and radiate, each in their own, characteristic way. Each molecule, comprising of thousands, even millions of atoms, vibrate, spin and radiate in their own particular way. Molecules and atoms can even be recognized based on their radiation. However, the smaller the scale, the harder it is to recognize our own particular features. The atoms, which described of consisting mostly of empty space, create the solid world that we observe. At the subatomic level, then, we are energy and vibration. All the material is actually mostly made up of empty space. Thus, at the subatomic level, we are something else than what we observe.

The whole universe can, therefore, be said to be a web of interconnected energy clusters. Is it even possible, observing on a particle level, to distinguish clearly where I end and where another person begins? Everything is interwoven, and we are connected with each other. As a matter of fact, we are all part of one and the same.

Quantum physics reverts back to the ideas of oriental philosophies regarding the interconnectedness of everything, unity and shared consciousness. Since in quantum physics, one deals with particles, one cannot draw the direct conclusion that the results would qualify when assessing everyday experiences. However, no hard upper limit to which the laws of quantum physics apply has been found as of yet. The results would seem to apply to even large systems. Therefore, it can well be the case that a researcher affects the results of experiments with his or her own thoughts, that an energy healer affects the results of a treatment, and that remote healing is possible.

CHAPTER 12. About the mind and consciousness

"The energy of the mind is the essence of life".
- Aristotle, philosopher (384-322 BCE)

The extraordinary development of natural sciences since the beginning of the modern era is often seen as a result of science becoming focused on the physical world, while the mind and the spirit were set aside. Understanding the world was attempted by trying to measure it quantitatively and physically. Lately, a need has been expressed to bring science and spirituality closer to each other again. Theories of natural science have been developed without the mind – without taking into account either its existence or its effect. Science is able to measure in detail only such things that are not mixed up with consciousness.

Changing perspectives

The *mind*, like *energy*, can be understood in many different ways. Some use it to refer to everything non-material that has to do with the human being. In other words everything else except the physical body. Often, the mind denotes just the subconscious mind and its processes, but sometimes also the conscious mind and reasoning. In the context of healing, one often refers to the subconscious, non-conscious mind. Compared to consciousness, the mind is something more individual: it is a person's inner, spiritual essence, where consciousness manifests itself along with thoughts and feelings. The philosopher David Chalmers defines *consciousness* as a subjective experience, that is, a human being or any other system is conscious, if it has some kind of sensation of what it feels like to be a thinking being. Also, consciousness is often used to refer to an entity that includes the sensations experienced and, in general, all possible attainable information.

Understanding the human mind and consciousness is an issue that holds many challenges and unanswered questions. The philosopher David Chalmers divides the questions related to consciousness into so-called easy problems, such as questions pertaining to the structure of the mind and the brain and how the brain processes information, and a so-called hard problem of consciousness. The hard problem of consciousness is more challenging: why do we have experiences (qualia) and why do experiences feel like something to us? There is a desire to explain why and how we experience subjective, conscious sensory experiences, and how different sensations have specific characteristics, such as pain, color, and taste. The human genome map has been almost completely determined, but if we would use the map to create a whole being, it would be unlikely that we would get a conscious, thinking human being, but rather a zombie without a mind. The research of consciousness is interdisciplinary, including physics, medicine, biology, philosophy ,and psychology, and there has been lots of development in recent years. Does our brain generate consciousness, or is our brain just a computer, an interface that mediates consciousness? The topic of consciousness is simultaneously familiar, and difficult to grasp and to describe. The on-going research and the data mounting up begin to point all the more strongly to the notion that the consciousness is not a product of the brain. Although we have a much better understanding of the problem of consciousness than years ago, Chalmers claims that we are still not any closer to resolving the hard problem of consciousness.

The mind-body problem stems from the 17th century separation of the religion and science. As a result of the division, the realm of science focused on describing the physical world. *Physicalism* claims that reality consists only of the physical world, and that everything can be explained through physics. Alongside physicalism, the word *materialism* is often used, with the notion that nothing else exists but matter and changes of that. The materialistic view is the predominant way to explain the world nowadays, because it is easy to grasp with everyday reasoning – after all, it explains a major part of our observed daily phenomena. Physicalism, however, does present a few challenges. Initially, physicalism was not even intended to explain the mind. In a way, it was already known that the model was not perfect, and the mind had to be fitted into it.

Physicalism focused on the physical world, and on things that could be examined through quantitative physical measurements. For instance, the movement, form and size of a body are characteristics that can be observed and measured objectively. Subjective experiences, such as the body's color, smell and sounds, were associated with the mind, and left out of the physical study. The subjective mental realm is, however, closely linked with the brain. Nowadays, the materialistic viewpoint does, indeed, explain the mind as a product of the brain, and all the things associated with the mind, including consciousness, as originating from the brain and its structure. The growth in popularity of the materialistic viewpoint has also been strongly affected by the development of the research equipment and methods: the biological and physical reality can be measured and studied with increasing accuracy. It is always possible to argue that more accurate measurements would explain the phenomena. However, the materialistic model cannot provide an answer to the most essential and basic question about consciousness: why experiences are there and how they are felt. With the materialistic model, it is possible to explain the brain's activity and behavior, but not to explain subjective experiences, or to even determine if such experiences exist. For instance, how does water feel or what does the color violet look like? Already at the time of the birth of materialism, the model was considered lacking. The philosopher and mathematician René Descartes, among others, claimed that both mind and matter were real, separate, and interacting with each other. This division has become known as Cartesian dualism.

In *dualism,* it is assumed that the realm of physics doesn't extend to mind. The mental level is thus not taken into account. *Idealism*, in turn, seeks to bring mind and matter together by explaining that consciousness and mind are the origins of the physical world. Idealism is related, among others, to the thoughts found in some Hindu and Buddhist philosophies. For instance, in Hinduism, consciousness, which flows from god, Brahman, is the source of all reality. Also Plato's thoughts in ancient Greece can be considered idealistic. Plato spoke of "ideas" or "forms" that were only "images" or "copies" of reality, perceived with our senses. The most accurate, purest reality is represented through non-physical forms, and observable with mental capacities. The influence of Plato, Aristotle and other Greek philosophers can still be seen in Western thinking. They sought, among others, to understand reality by rational means: that which truly *is*, i.e., the real form. Forms are unchanging and perfect. It follows from this that the world that we observe with our senses and that is ever-changing, is not pure reality, but only an illusion created by our senses. We arrive, then, to the same notion that quantum physics came to later on: our observations affect the measurements. Plato also thought that from pure reality follows everything else, that is, pure reality is also unity, or one. In unity resides a perfect logical order, and it is possible to strive for pure reality by rational means. This concept would lead, at the time, to the further development of mathematics.

Around the time of the development of quantum physics, philosophy was strongly influenced by *positivism*. Part of positivism was the emphasis on the importance given to sensory perceptions in science. Observations were a starting point for research, and the role of science was to place observations within the unified theories. Emphasis was also placed on accuracy: concepts needed to be presented accurately, and to be applied to observations through theories. Positivism also had a strong impact on the birth of quantum physics.

The views of Einstein and Pauli, in particular, were also influenced by realism, and both sought to understand reality. Nowadays, *realism* refers to describing the world independently from the observer and their consciousness. Thus, according to realism, our world exists whether we observe it or not. The way of thinking is similar to how we might think in everyday life. Indeed, realism is close to materialism. In addition to these philosophies, there are other views that seek to explain the issue of consciousness, among them behaviorism and functionalism. The theories seek to find a connection between the mental and the material world, but they don't take a stand on the issue of subjective experiences.

Above, I have presented some of the most general views on the issue and realm of consciousness. Reality is actually more complicated than this. Among others, the philosopher David Bohm, one of the physicists who have interpreted quantum physics, dismissed materialism and emphasized holism or nonseparability - the undivided unity and qualitative infinity of the universe. In other words, Bohm ended up stating in his ontology that spirit and matter are fundamentally part of the same neutral entity, meaning that they are neither spirit (idealism) or matter (materialism), nor spirit and matter (dualism).

What, then, does all of this suggest? There are different views on the issue of the mind and consciousness. The way we look at our everyday life is not necessarily the "right" model by which to describe the whole reality. In his book *Science Delusion,* the biologist Rupert Sheldrake divides the current, dominant worldview roughly into ten dogmas, which he then proceeds to disprove one after the other. According to the prevailing model, the universe as well as we, human beings, are like machines, just matter devoid of consciousness. Your genes determine your future, and your memories as well as your mind are held in your brain. It follows from this that the phenomena classified as paranormal such as telepathy are impossible, and likewise, it is not possible for thoughts and intentions to have an effect from a distance.

From time to time, a certain model can rise to become the dominant one, but it shouldn't be allowed to restrict thinking. Models are just attempts to describe reality. However, reality is something else, and at times it is necessary to shake the prevailing models and assumptions. It is perfectly possible to use several models to describe the whole reality, and this can require changing one's own approach and way of thinking. Wolfgang Pauli, who played an important role in interpreting quantum physics, collaborated closely with Carl Jung on the interpretation of dreams, as, in addition to physics, Pauli relied strongly on psychology. In his letter to Abraham Pais, Pauli states: "*It is my personal opinion that in the science of the future, reality will neither be "psychic" nor "physical" but somehow both and somehow neither.*"

In his book *Mind and Cosmos*, Thomas Nagel claims that the best that we can do is to develop alternative views with which to describe each important field as well as possible. Nagel challenges particularly the devoted materialists and Darwinists to expand the boundaries of thinking in the light of how little we actually understand the world and its phenomena, not to mention ourselves. It is necessary to make experiments deviating from our accepted models and to seek answers even from unexpected directions. Science rarely achieves big leaps by simply adapting customary models with small changes. Often, the most significant leaps of development have stemmed from unexpected, even imaginary directions. Maybe this implies, that perhaps we aren't ever able to reach the truth just because of the limitations of our own understanding. Nagel claims that it still makes sense to look for an all-encompassing answer to how we are placed in the world. Science will likely never come to a joint agreement that gaining a more detailed view of the world isn't possible. We are just at the beginning: we have, for instance, just begun to admit that there are phenomena related to the mind that cannot be understood with our current scientific models. Through the study of such phenomena, it is possible to gain precious information that will help us understand the whole.

At school and in our everyday lives, as we grow, we learn to adopt a materialistic worldview. However, this view is limiting. Reality cannot be thought of as just matter. Subjective experiences cannot be left out of the picture. They are needed for us to understand the world. Furthermore, they bring a spiritual element to reality. Reality is made up of both physical and spiritual elements. When we understand the role of spirituality as a part of reality, our concept of reality is transformed and our perspective expanded. The observer creates the reality, and the materialistic world is only an illusion. To quote the physicist Sir James Jeans:

> "The stream of knowledge is heading toward a non-mechanical reality; the universe begins to look more like a great thought than like a great machine. Mind no longer appears to be an accidental intruder into the realm of matter, we ought rather hail it as the creator and governor of the realm of matter."

From R.C. Henry's text "The Mental Universe," *Nature* 436:29, 2005

The different views on the topic of consciousness made me realize that I don't need to adapt my own experiences to fit a materialistic view that has challenges in explaining subjective experience. In energy healing

169

there is, inevitably, a spiritual element, and a different kind of view might be better suited. This doesn't mean that the materialistic view is wrong. Perhaps it just isn't the best-suited model to describe energy healing. Opposites are complementary, as the saying goes in quantum physics.

Mind and matter

Can the mind affect matter? According to quantum physics, yes it can. One could even say that the observer creates the reality that they observe with their consciousness. According to quantum physics, the entire universe is vibrating energy. Our entire physical world, and all matter, is energy. Therefore thoughts and feelings, and the mind are also energy. The answer to the mind-matter problem can be found in the particle-wave dualism of the double slit experiment. Dr. Dean Radin, Chief Scientist of the Institute of Noetic Sciences (IONS), has studied the connection between consciousness and the physical reality with double-slit experiments. In the study, he examined the effect of the observer's attention on the results obtained. As predicted, As predicted, directing human consciousness to a physical measurement changed the measured outcome of the experiment.

The evidence is mounting up that the mind affects matter. Among such interesting studies, which point to that, are the random number generator measurements of the PEAR (Princeton Engineering Anomalies Research) research project. The research was conducted at Princeton University as an international collaboration starting already in 1979 and lasting for decades. The aim of the project was to study the hypothesis that human consciousness has a direct affect on physical equipment. Usually, random number generators   generate numbers zero and one randomly. However, the data provided by random number generators placed around the world showed that when a group of people focuses their attention on a common thing, the random number generators actually no longer provide numbers as randomly. Plenty of examples of such anomalies in measurements have been accumulated in the course of the years. Such events have been, for instance, the tsunami on the Indian Ocean on December 26th, 2004, 9/11 in 2001, and Princess Diana's death on August 31st, 1997. In these instances, as in others, the random number generators started to diverge considerably from the random a few hours before the events. The database collected during 28 years of operation of the research project in question clearly proves that thoughts and feelings have an effect on the physical reality and that this can also be measured.

The Japanese doctor Masaru Emoto has conducted research on the effect of human consciousness on the molecular structure of water. There has been a particular interest in water studies because human beings are made of 70% water. The effect of thoughts on water was studied by crystallizing water to ice crystals and by examining the differences between them. It has been repeatedly disclosed that positive thoughts create symmetrical, well-formed crystals, whereas negative thoughts produce asymmetrical, formless crystals. The experiment has been repeated many times. Once, Emoto and Radin arranged an experiment in which 1900 people from Austria and Germany focused their thoughts for three consecutive days on water samples that were kept in an electromagnetically protected room in California. The water samples were located close to control water bowls, but the experiment participants didn't know about this. In addition, samples were kept outside the protected room. Ice crystals were formed from the water, and they were photographed. The photos were assessed by a group of 2500 impartial outsiders. Their conclusion was that the water samples thought with purpose created more beautiful crystals than those in the control samples. The experiment confirmed the results of previous pilot studies. One variant of the water experiments is also Masaru Emoto's rice experiment, which can be performed at home, too. In Emoto's rice experiment, boiled rice is placed in two different jars. One jar is labeled with "love" and the other with "hate". Positive feelings and love are then directed to the jar labeled love and negative feelings and hate toward the hate-jar. As the experiment goes on, it happens that the rice in the hate-jar gets quickly moldy, whereas the rice in the love-jar keeps well for a long time. Emoto has also discovered that if a third jar is added to the experiment, and is not paid any attention to, the rice in the third jar gets moldy even faster than the rice in the hate-jar. According to the experiment, the worst thing is to leave something completely without attention, as if it didn't exist at all.

The mind and healing

The power of the mind is immense, often much greater than we realize. The mind affects physiology in many ways, as we already know from stress, among others. It is also known than the mind has an effect on healing. Many medical studies on the placebo effect indicate that the power of the mind is even so great that the belief in healing is of much more importance than the actual treatment that one receives.

It is often assumed that energy healing, too, is based on some form of belief on the effect of the treatment. However, for the time being, there would not seem to be a single, unified view of the effect of belief on healing. In Bengston's research, skeptical healers were able to heal mice, once they had learned the method. In Grad's research, in turn, skeptical medical students who were treating mice obtained slower healing results than those in the control group. In his research, Benor also claims that skepticism could slow down the effect of the treatment. Kieger, on the other hand, states in his publication related to the TT method that belief in the efficiency of the treatment did not seem to influence its effect.

In her book *Mind over Medicine – Scientific proof you can heal yourself,* doctor Lissa Rankin deals with how the mind and body work. The body cannot differentiate, for instance, between the causes for stress: it experiences work-related stress, the stress caused by health problems and the stress stemming from family relationships in the same way. The mind reacts to these in a similar way. The power of the mind can make a person healthy. A person can heal from even difficult states if only they have faith, even when medicine suggests differently. This is placebo. People have the tendency to heal no matter what treatment is given, as long as they consider the treatment efficient. Often placebo is mistakenly thought of as a fake effect, which doesn't give adequate credit to the phenomenon, as it suggests that there is no effect at all. Placebo effect can, however, be quite considerable, and it can also be measured. Placebo indicates that there is indeed a connection between mind and body. Patients treated with placebo don't just feel better but actually heal from warts, infections, emphysema and tumors. There is

173

ample research data on such measurable, physiological phenomena. It is also known that there is an opposite effect to placebo, called nocebo and that one can make oneself ill. When a patient is given an injection and told that it is chemotherapy, they vomit and loose their hair. Negative expectations have a negative effect on the treatment result and on health.

It does not even seem to matter whether a person is aware of receiving just placebo; it still works. Ted Kaptchuk, professor of medicine and director of the Program of Placebo Studies and the Therapeutic Encounter at Harvard Medical School, and his group demonstrated that it isn't even necessary to fool patients in order for placebo to work. In the experiment, 80 patients with IBS or Irritable Bowel Syndrome were either given placebo or didn't receive any treatment. Patients in the placebo group were told that they were receiving placebo medicine and that placebo often had an effect on healing. They were also told that they didn't need to believe in the effect of the placebo, but that they still had to take the medicine. After three weeks, the patients of the placebo group, while aware of receiving placebo, described their symptoms as having eased as much as two times more compared to the group that didn't receive treatment. According to Kaptchuk, the difference was so significant as to be comparable to the improvement caused by the best medicine designed for IBS. Ted Kaptchuk considers expectations to be important. Even though those treated in a research program receive placebo, they are part of a positive atmosphere and of an innovative approach, and positivity is contagious. Furthermore, during the treatment, they also develop the daily ritual of taking a pill, which creates an atmosphere conducive to change. In other words, they direct their attention toward healing. Kaptchuk's research group aims to find the means to strengthen the placebo effect, which is quite exceptional, as usually in research, there is an attempt to eliminate the placebo effect. So far, placebo control has been utilized mostly in pharmaceutical tests. Pharmaceutical companies need to be able to demonstrate that in addition to having the desired effect, the effects of medicine are considerably better than those in the placebo group, as healing takes place in both groups. The results of the research conducted by Kaptchuk's group were published in the peer-reviewed medical publication *PLOS*.

While the existence of placebo is a generally accepted fact and while it is exploited, there is no clear idea about how placebo works and what the underlying mechanism of action is. There are subconscious processes related to healing, such as the functioning of the immune system, and it isn't always clear what affects them. Sometimes the mere sight of a doctor's white coat is enough to initiate healing, at other times taking an expensive enough pill. In Espay et al.'s placebo research, the effect of the cost of medicine in the treatment of Parkinson's disease was studied. It was shown that the ability to move among those who had taken an expensive medicine had improved more than those who had taken a cheaper medicine, while both groups had been given the placebo.

Radin and Lobach present an interesting viewpoint on placebo in their publication "Toward Understanding the Placebo Effect: Investigating a Possible Retrocausal Factor": what if improvement was caused by the goal-oriented nature of placebo, meaning that placebo could be explained teleologically? Thus, the expectation of the future would direct our attention to what will possibly be realized, and attention will unconsciously lead to a certain direction. Based on Radin and Lobach's research and the earlier research conducted on related topics, it would seem that humans have a subconscious ability to foresee the future, and further research would be required to find out how the subconscious expectation affects the body and the mind, and if this could help explain placebo, too.

In his book *The Distinction of Past and Future, from the Character of Physical Law* dating from 1965, the physicist Richard Feynman states the following:

> *"If the world of nature is made of atoms, and we too are made of atoms and obey physical laws, the most obvious interpretation of this evident distinction between past and future, and this irreversibility of all phenomena, would be that some laws, some of the motion laws of the atoms, are going one way - that the atom laws are not such that they can go either way. There should be somewhere in the works some kind of a principle that uxles only make wuxles, and never vice versa, and so the world is turning from uxley character to wuxley character all the time - and this one-way business of the interactions of things should be the thing that makes the whole phenomena of the world seem to go one way. But we have not found this yet. That is, in all the laws of physics that we have found so far there does not seem to be any distinction between the past and the future. The moving picture should*

work the same going both ways, and the physicist who looks at it should not laugh."

Doctor Larry Dossey, who for years has worked as a pioneer in matters pertaining to the mind, spirituality and healing, suggests that non-local healing bears the effect of the non-local mind. By non-local he means through his or her thoughts or intentions, a person could have an effect on another person from a distance, beyond the reach of the senses, even when the person at a distance is unaware of the intention. Remote healing and prayer, for instance, are such activities. Various hypotheses, that could explain the transfer of energy or information, have been presented to explain remote healing, based, among others, on quantum entanglement, holography, complementarity, quantum vacuums, zero-point energy, and the physiology of microtubules. There is still a lot to research to be done on the topic of healing. So far, Sir Arthur Eddington's comment on the complementarity of modern physics might best serve to describe the situation related to healing and consciousness: *"Something unknown is doing we don't know what."*

WHAT KIND OF STUDIES HAVE BEEN DONE ON ENERGY HEALING?

CHAPTER 13. Energy healing studies

"Science, my boy, is made up of mistakes, but they are mistakes which it is useful to make, because they lead little by little to the truth."
- Jules Verne, Journey to the Center of the Earth

Research is today's adventure. And what could be more rewarding than researching a topic that isn't so well known. What do existing studies tell about energy healing? I myself was eagerly conducting preliminary research as well.

What can energy healing be helpful for?

So far, there has not been much experimental research on energy healing, although energy treatments have been in use throughout the world for thousands of years. Results of energy healing research are published in several publication series that are focused on health and well-being. Among peer-reviewed publication series focused specifically on the topic of energy healing are the *Journal of Alternative and Comprehensive Medicine, the Journal of Scientific Exploration, Alternative Therapies in Health, and Medicine,* and *Explore: The Journal of Science and Healing.* The research that I refer to in this chapter is either published in peer-reviewed journals or on reliable, impartial websites collecting energy healing results.

The research on energy healing is, in practice, currently divided into two areas: clinical research studying the effects of energy healing, and research on subtle energy – the energy flowing from the hands – and fields, and verifying that such fields exist. The majority of the research conducted in the past 50 years has focused on researching whether the phenomenon is real. The research on the effects of healing has mainly focused on supporting the healing of various symptoms, ailments and illnesses, on pain relief and on well-being in general.

Nowadays, the increasingly accurate measuring devices enable us to gain more detailed information about ourselves, too. Over the last hundred years, medicine has made increasing use of various kinds of equipment that serve to measure human biofields. With biofields I refer to the fields around and inside the body such as, for instance, the temperature field created by the body's temperature, or the gravitation field caused by mass. Currently, there is a special focus and interest, in medicine, on the body's electromagnetic field, as this can be easily measured. Research on the heart's energy field began about a hundred years ago, and around the same period, the brain's electric field was measured for the first time, leading to the development of the electroencephalogram, or EEG. The heart's electrical activity, in turn, is measured with the electrocardiogram, or ECG. Also, both the brain's and the heart's magnetic characteristics can be measured. Nowadays it is known that of the human organs, the heart emits the strongest electromagnetic radiation. The amplitude of the electrocardiogram (ECG) is 60 times greater than the amplitude of the electroencephalogram (EEG). The magnetic field created by the heart is as much as 5000 times stronger than that of the brain. Also the magnetic characteristics of tissues, muscles and, for instance, the electrical activity or magnetic characteristics of the eye's retina can be measured.

The challenge in measuring the human body is in the very low readings, and it isn't until recent decades that sufficiently accurate equipment has been available, permitting these measurements. For instance, the extremely sensitive magnetometer SQUID (Superconducting Quantum Interference Device) can be used to measure the changes in the magnetic field of tissues. SQUID has also been useful for energy healing research.

Most commonly, the effect of energy healing is examined by observing changes occurring in the body and by measuring various numerical values related to the body's activities. The body's reactions can be measured, but information on subjective experiences can only be retrieved through research based on surveys. Information on the mind's activity during a treatment can be obtained by doing research on the brain or the bodily reactions. The EEG allows getting information on the brain's activity and reactions. By examining several similar cases, it is possible to find out, for instance, how focusing or relaxing can be seen in the brain. It is possible to measure the pulse and the heart rate variability, which also tell about relaxation or the stress level. The heart rate variability measures the variations between consecutive heartbeats.

In energy healing research, the TT (Therapeutic Touch) method, the HT (Healing Touch) method, Reiki, and some other remote healing methods such as prayer are often compiled together. The HT method is a form of the TT method. Even though both methods' names mention touch, neither method necessarily involves touching. Instead, the treatment is mostly given by holding hands at some distance from the body, and by cleansing and bringing energy to the body with movements of the hands. TT originated in the 1970s, when professor Dolores Krieger from New York University, and the healer Dora Kunz studied Oskar Estebany's work and brought their own observations to support the healing.

Energy healing research is often criticized for its quality. When conducting research on the effect of energy healing, comparative research of a sufficiently high quality is required including randomized double blind studies. In randomized double blind studies the patients are divided randomly into a group of treated patients, and a control group, whose members either don't receive any treatment or receive some other treatment. What makes this a double blind study is that neither the members of the two groups nor the researchers themselves know, who belongs to which group, who receives proper treatment and who gets placebo. The blind study is conducted to eliminate the effect of suggestion on the results. The randomized double blind study enables to find out whether the method used is significantly more effective than placebo.

Most research on energy healing has taken place in the United States, where it is also available as a complementary form of treatment for instance in hospitals. In its project in 2012, The Institute of Noetic Sciences (IONS) compiled together the study results of several energy healing methods. With reference to energy healing, both a summarizing article published by IONS and articles published by the North American Centre for Complementary and Alternative Medicine (NCCAM) point out that the existing research is insufficient to allow drawing real conclusions about their effects. There is a need for systematic, all-encompassing and sufficiently high-quality research. The summarizing article by IONS voices criticism regarding the quality of existing research: research always ought to include a sufficiently detailed description of the method used, the healer's experience, the duration of the treatment, and both the healer's and the patient's observations during the treatment. However, the article points out that while energy healing lack a joint definition and that therefore, drawing final conclusions is impossible, consistent changes have been observed among the values obtained from energy healing research. Among these are changes in a patient's heartbeat, hemoglobin and hematocrit values, as well as in their diastolic blood pressure. (Hematocrit: the ratio of the volume of red blood cells to the total volume of blood. In conditions of stress, the hematocrit increases.) However, the summary states that the underlying reason could actually be the body's reaction to the healer's touch and the effect of relaxation. The decrease of the stress symptoms and the changes in the blood pressure would seem to recur in observations made in other studies. Vitale's research also found an effect on the healing of wounds. Research on the effect of energy healing on pain relief has also taken place, but it is not possible to draw general conclusions based on this yet. In any case, good results have been gained from the effect of energy healing on pain relief, for instance in connection with teeth drilling and with cancer patients.

Miles and True compiled together the existing research on Reiki. Their studies showed, among others, significant pain relief during treatments, as well as a normalizing of the blood's glucose values with people whose values were at an abnormal level. Research related to the healing of wounds showed a clearly accelerated rate of healing among the energy healing patients. However, it is impossible to make definitive conclusions based on this due to the fairly small groups and some factors that changed during the study. In the research on treatment following heart attacks, the mood among those who had received Reiki treatment was somewhat better, and more positive emotions were experienced than among the control group. Information on the development following the treatments is, however, not available, so it is not possible to estimate the long-term effects. The influence of Reiki on mood was also observed in Wardell and Engebretson's research, in which Reiki was shown to considerably diminish anxiety, lower systolic blood pressure and, in addition, lower the EMG (electromyography) values. EMG measures electric phenomena related to muscle activity and shows relaxation occurring during the treatment. Miles and True note that even though there are only a few high quality and comprehensive studies conducted to-date on energy healing, it is important to share the observations gained so as to direct further research toward the relevant areas. The documented treatment cases, the research describing energy healing and the randomized research, although made so far for groups that are too small, together gradually increase the understanding of energy healing.

Mapping the results of energy healing studies

To help gain a better understanding of both my own and my patients' experiences, I compiled some research observations on the effects of energy healing in different cases. In practice, the research shows some common observations such as deep relaxation, pain relief in various acute and chronic pain conditions, relief of anxiety, and mood improvement. Changes have been observed particularly in values measuring stress, among these the heartbeat, blood pressure, cortisol, muscle tension, values related to the body's oxygen intake or hemoglobin, hematocrit values, and the blood's glucose values. However, the results cannot be generalized yet; further research is required.

Effect on the mood and well-being

The effect of energy healing on the mood and well-being has mostly been investigated through comparative research, such as Bowden et al's research, which examined the effect of Reiki on a group of 40 University students who had experienced symptoms of depression. Half of the students were given Reiki and half just relaxation treatment, altogether 6 treatment sessions lasting 30 minutes each in the course of a five-week follow-up period. The group that received Reiki reported about a clear mood improvement and a decrease in stress symptoms, whereas in the other group, no such changes were observed.

Often in Reiki research, the control group receives "fake Reiki", in other words their healers copy Reiki healing positions, but haven't actually received training to give Reiki or the activations involved in Reiki healing. It is common for the control group receiving "fake Reiki" to show statistically significant deviations in their feeling of well-being compared to the control group that doesn't receive any treatment. This happened also, for instance, in Catlin et al.'s double blind study, in which 189 patients were divided into three separate groups: both in the groups receiving Reiki and "fake Reiki", well-being improved in comparison to normal medical treatment. An added note: Bengston suggested that in the reported placebo cases, what was actually at stake could be a resonant bonding between the different groups.

In Shore's double blind study, 45 participants received treatment to relieve depression and stress symptoms. Each participant was chosen randomly to partake in a group receiving alternatively Reiki healing, remote healing, placebo Reiki, or remote-placebo Reiki treatment. They received treatment for 1-1,5 hours at a time for six weeks. Again, in the placebo groups, the healers just copied the Reiki positions without actually knowing how Reiki healing is done. The patients' stress levels were measured in different surveys. The tests administered before the research showed that there was no difference between the patient groups. In the tests administered after the treatment regimen, however, there was a significant difference between both the Reiki and placebo Reiki groups, and the remote Reiki and remote placebo Reiki groups. The researchers performed the same tests again a year after the initial research, and the difference between the groups remained the same. The differences between the groups disappeared, however, when the groups that had received placebo Reiki were also given Reiki healing following the research. It would be interesting to repeat a similar research once again among an even larger group of patients. According to Shore's research, it would seem that Reiki has an effect of improving well-being also when observed over a longer timeframe. I have also received similar feedback from my own patients.

Pain relief and cancer

In my experience, energy healing relieves pain. The majority of the research on energy healing has indeed been conducted on the subject of pain, especially in the case of cancer patients. Research has shown that energy healing relieves both acute and chronic pain, is useful in relaxing, helps tiredness and generally increases well-being. For instance, in Birocco et al.'s research, which involved the study of 118 cancer patients, who were given four treatment sessions lasting 30 minutes each, the patients reported about mood improvement, relaxation, pain relief, improved quality of sleep, and relief of anxiety. Good results have also been obtained in the case of arthritis, and generally regarding the mobility of the joints.

Due to my experience treating Melli, I was naturally interested in existing cancer research. Gronowicz et al. observed mice that had been injected with breast cancer, just as in Bengston's research. The research indicates that the TT method utilized has a significant effect on breast cancer's metastases and on the immune response. In their research, the metastases decreased in size, but the actual tumor remained intact.

There was no research available where patients had received energy healing before other treatments, or among patients who had refused to take on medical treatment. Instead, several studies could be found, where cancer patients were given energy healing to support other treatment. Jain et al.'s article compiles together clinical studies that have been conducted among cancer patients both concurrently with traditional Western treatments, and after them. They observed relief of depression, decrease in fatigue, and changes in some clinically significant, biological measurement values, such as cortisol. However, all studies didn't show change for the better. Some studies mentioned the slowing down of the division of cancer cells, and the obstruction of DNA synthesis. In their summarizing article, Jain et al. state that these promising, preliminary results call for further research. Most proof of the effect of energy healing would seem to exist specifically in the case of pain and cancer, which have been researched the most. Good results have also been obtained in the case of arthritis, dementia and heart diseases. As a matter of fact, in Garland et al.'s research, it was cancer patients who reported having benefited the most from energy healing compared to other, complementary treatments. Also their research calls for further investigation.

Effect on the healer

Many healers experience energy healing in their own body as well through relaxation and various bodily sensations. The physical changes that occur in the healers during the treatment have been researched for decades, but it has not been possible to detect unambiguous, uniform, clear changes to-date. In an article published in 2015, Baldwin et al. measured the healers' electroencephalogram (EEG) and heart rate variability. The EEG results varied inconsistently, which is why one could not draw conclusions from them. According to the heart rate variability results, some forms of energy healing (Reconnective Healing, Bruyere healing, Hawaian healing) showed slight physiological

187

changes, but in the case of Reiki and the TT method (Therapeutic Touch), this didn't occur. No long-term studies on the effect of energy healing on the well-being of healers have been carried out yet.

Healing of wounds

Already in the research done in the 1960s, Bernard Grad noticed that the energy healer could significantly speed up the healing of wounds in mice. Wirth et al., for instance, have conducted preliminary studies related to the speeding up of the healing of wounds. In their studies, the healing of biopsy wounds in healthy people was examined, but it isn't possible to make final conclusions based on the results. In part of the studies, noticeable healing was observed in a group that received treatment, whereas part of the studies showed no effect, or even the opposite. They believe that the results were affected, among others, by the fact that the investigated groups were incommensurable. In addition, they mention that the research assistant had taken part in every group's research, which may have affected the results. Thus further research is required. Research that would study the effect of the energy treatment on the healing of different types of wounds was not found.

Spiritual growth

Reiki, among others, was originally developed as a tool for supporting spiritual growth. In the case of my own patients, I noticed that within a year of the start of my treatments, as much as 85% of my patients would also become interested in learning a method related to spiritual growth, or had learned or started learning energy healing. Dr. Daniel J. Benor's summarizing research states that energy healing has often been associated with the increase of spiritual consciousness. Among the challenges of research on spiritual growth is the issue of how to systematically define spiritual growth. It is also challenging to define,

189

which of the observed changes are a result of the treatment, and which are due to something else. The effect of regular energy healing, or generally the effect on well-being and health, such as improved self-confidence and self-expression, or the opening and development of a spiritual connection, is hard to measure other than through surveys.

The touch

I personally treat my patients according to my intuition either by holding my hands a few inches away from the body or by touching lightly. Often I might treat especially the area of the head by holding my hands slightly over the patient's body. In my own experience, I will feel the treatment even more strongly when my hands are slightly away from the body than when I am touching it.

It seems that patients cannot, at least consciously, distinguish between a Reiki treatment and placebo Reiki, for instance. This was also found in the studies conducted by Dr. Ahlam A. Mansour, and Dr. Zimmermann. However, I suspect that the groups that they studied were incommensurable. Mansour, among others, studied Reiki healers, and healers who were taught Reiki, but who didn't receive Reiki activations. In other words, did they actually just study the results among Reiki healers? In my experience, the ability to give energy healing is strengthened simply by getting energy healing. Strictly speaking, the activations are considered to be a part of learning Reiki; their purpose is to strengthen the connection to the source of universal life energy and to help channel the energy. However, it would be interesting to study the difference between experienced Reiki healers, those who have done Reiki for a few months, those who have just attended a Reiki course, and those who don't know Reiki. According to my own, and many other healers' experience, the heat radiating from the hands gets stronger, the more Reiki one has done. Also, for instance when giving joint healing together with my students, the patient can recognize, based on the level of heat, which part of the body I am treating. The body learns to act in a certain way during the healing. Would it be possible to obtain a difference in the feeling of heat stemming from the hands also in the case of other healers?

Touch can, however, be a significant element in helping create a connection in a healing situation. Touch stimulates the skin's pressure receptors, thus lowering stress hormone levels and stimulating oxytocin secretion, which increases the feeling of confidence and connection. Touch has been studied among NBA basketball players, among others, and it has been observed that the amount of touch from team players at the start of the season correlates directly with the team's success toward the end of the season. In a fast game, there is little time for discussion, but touch is a means to establish a connection and to transmit information.

In research where the difference between authentic treatment and placebo treatment has been studied, positive effects have often been found in the placebo treatment group, compared to the group that doesn't receive any treatment. This would indicate that such factors as the healer's presence, support, attention, touch, and the patient's possible sense of the healer's capability and healing intention, would have at least some importance on the positive outcome of the treatment. Research on remote healing can further increase the understanding of the effect of the healer's presence.

Research on remote healing

Remote influencing or remote healing is part of many energy healing methods, such as Reiki, the Therapeutic Touch method, qigong, Pranic healing, and Bengston's method. Praying, too, is remote influencing. Each of these has its own approach, whereby a person affects another person from a distance, with the hope of creating change. Remote healing is one of the most commonly used forms of complementary treatment, although there is no undeniable scientific evidence of its effect. Clinical research has provided contradictory results. One likely reason for the contradictions is that there are variables related to remote influencing, which haven't been recognized, whose behavior isn't understood or cannot be controlled. The mere number of people partaking in remote healing creates challenges. The healer has his or her own intention, the wish for the treatment's effect. There is also patient's own intention, which isn't necessarily the same as the healer's. In remote healing research, those conducting the study have their own expectations regarding the progress of the research, as do all the others who know about the research, read about it in a research article, and so on. How can everyone's influence be taken into account in the research? This is why studies have focused on some basic questions underlying remote healing. Is it possible, for instance, to influence a living system at a distance by means of an intention and thoughts alone? In addition to providing answers to the question of effectiveness, the research could also help find answers to questions such as, how often, for how long, and for how long at a time, remote healing should be given so as to be as efficient as possible.

The effect of remote healing has been compared to simple life forms, fungi, bacteria, enzymes, yeast, cells, animals and human beings. Benor compiled together the results of several studies on remote healing. In the summary, the methodological quality of 50 studies is deemed excellent, and of these, 74% (37) are estimated to have produced statistically significant results and proof of the influence of remote healing.

Clinical studies have shown the influence of remote healing on the sympathetic nervous system - also known as the "fight or flight" response describing the body's reaction to stress or danger – when a remote healer has strived to affect a person located in a different space, causing alternately tension and relaxation. Astin et al. compiled together randomized double blind studies related to the clinical remote healing studies, and described the results of 23 tests including 2774 patients as participants. In a total of 13 experiments out of 23, in other words 57% of them, statistically significant results were obtained; in 9 experiments a large enough difference to the control group was not observed, and in one experiment, the result was negative. In their publication, the researchers list many factors that may have affected the results, such as insufficient practice of the method or randomization in the formation of the groups – issues that are common in experiments involving healing, and similar type experiments. Astin et al. state that further research on the subject is needed.

In their publication about remote healing studies conducted in 2015, Radin et al. state that significant experimental observations have already been made. Dr. Dean Radin has compiled on his homepage a list of some of most significant remote healing studies published in peer-reviewed journals; the length of a comprehensive list would include thousands of articles. Radin et al. bring up challenges of remote healing research, such as studying the effect of the healing in practice. Measuring equipment is among the challenges of remote healing research. The measuring method needs to be capable of measuring and verifying phenomena as a whole. One challenge may well be posed by the incapability of current research methods to detect everything that occurs in this phenomenon. In laboratory studies, where the effect of remote healing has been studied to some specific values, or so-called DMILS (distant mental interactions with living systems), changes have been observed most clearly. Thus, we would also need to gain a better understanding of the theoretical background, of the non-local phenomena, and of the activity of the mind underlying remote healing.

Can the energy flowing from the hands be measured?

Since I first started to give energy healing, I have often bumped into questions about the energy flowing from hands. Does energy really flow from the hands? What is it, and can it be measured? Is it just heat? Based on my own experience, the most important part of the work in energy healing is performed at a mental level, but for both the healer and the healee, the heat of the hands is the most tangible sign that something is happening. It is also easiest to approach the changes that occur in the hands during the treatment.

There have been attempts to measure the energy streams possibly flowing from the healers' hands in energy treatments. Measurements have been done using a variety of instruments and methods and increasingly accurate equipment, such as magnetometers, voltmeters, photometers, gamma radiation counters, sound equipment and gas discharge visualization. Mostly, the research has focused on measuring electric and magnetic properties, because measuring them is fairly easy and electromagnetism is well understood.

Dr. James L. Oschmann, one of the pioneers of energy healing research, has studied the possible electric and magnetic characteristics of energy healing. He has presented a hypothesis on how energy healing works. Oschmann's hypothesis on the function of energy treatments is based on one of the basic laws in physics, Ampère's law, which states that when an electric current flows through a conductor, a magnetic field forms around it. If living tissues, muscles and organs conduct electricity, then, according to the laws of physics, a magnetic field is formed around the body. Conductivity in the body is, however, so weak that very accurate devices are required to measure the magnetic field, such as the SQUID superconducting quantum interference device. According to Oschmann's hypothesis, when an energy healer begins the treatment, the electromagnetic field of the healer's heart is strengthened. This information is transmitted to the healer's hands, which electromagnetic field can induce a flow into the tissues and cells of a person nearby. Oschmann estimates that the energy fields formed during treatments are small, and very precisely at a certain frequency that activates, among others, the body's immune system. However, this hypothesis doesn't explain remote healing.

Also Dr. John Zimmermann and Dr. Akira Seto have studied energy flows and fields stemming from the hands, referred to as "pulsating biomagnetic fields". Zimmermann studied extra low frequency (ELF) electromagnetic signals and discovered a difference between healers and non-healers. In a research dating from the 1970s, it was observed that magnetic fields could stimulate a growth process in bone fractures that were slow to heal. In 1979 FDA (US Food and Drug Administration) accepted the pulsed electromagnetic field therapy (PEMF) to help heal bones. In PEMF, a small pulse generator connected to a coil is placed close to a fracture that typically has not healed within 3-6 months, producing a magnetic field that induces currents to flow in nearby tissues.

The frequency level is about 7 Hz. Optimal frequencies for stimulating the healing of human tissue are all within ELF. Zimmermann studied the frequencies of healers' hands and noted that the frequencies of the signals in the healers' hands varied within a frequency range that has been found to stimulate the healing process most efficiently. The frequencies were at the same range as the brain waves. The frequency that occurred most often in the energy healers' hands was 7-8 Hz, or the alpha state. It is the same frequency range that has been found to stimulate the healing of tissues in other studies. Physiotherapy equipment based on these principles has been designed to help repair soft tissues. In other words, the frequencies measured in the energy healers' hands are, according to these studies, on a frequency range that is optimal for stimulating the healing of tissues.

Also Hisamitsu et al., Seto et al., and Moga and Bengston have observed changes in the magnetic fields during treatments. Changes were found on the site that the healer targeted his attention to. Significant changes didn't occur close to the healer in other researchers' studies, only Sidorov would note that unusual electromagnetic signals were detected in the vicinity of both the healer and the healee. Seto et al., in turn, observed in their study of qigong healers as they were treating patients that the strength of the magnetic field grew exceptionally and became even a thousand-times greater than the normal one. Changes in the magnetic fields were found in remote healing in addition to local healing. Similar changes in the vicinity of the objects have also been found in *remote viewing* research. Remote viewing is a technique that was developed for the needs of the US army in the 1970s. The technique involves quieting the logical, conscious mind and trusting intuition and the ability of the subconscious, unconscious mind to produce information. The information can be viewed independently of time and place; in other words, non-local information can be sought.

Professor Gary Schwartz et al. has measured the energy fields of the hands, and of the heart area, of energy healers. In the original research ca. 20 years ago, a difference was found between Reiki healers and healers who gave placebo. In addition, the research found that energy decreased as a function of distance. In his most recent studies, conducted with Baldwin, Schwartz used more accurate equipment, but the same phenomenon didn't occur. The researchers actually claimed that the practice of Reiki would not seem to routinely produce a high-intensity electromagnetic field from the heart or the hands of healers. The test arrangement was, however, not identical to the first one, as in the most recent experiment, the effect of external fields, such as the earth's magnetic field, was excluded. They went on to suggest that it could be possible that energy healing is stimulated by tuning into the external environmental radiation, such as the Schumann resonance. Due to the strong magnetic shielding surrounding the SQUID measuring equipment, it was impossible to study the mechanism in their experiments.

The Schumann resonances are a global electromagnetic resonance phenomenon occurring in the extremely low frequency (ELF) band of the Earth's electromagnetic field spectrum. In the resonance, the system's vibration gains strength in the vicinity of its natural frequency or resonant frequency, just like when plucking a guitar string: the sound is produced by the string's resonance frequencies. The fundamental frequency of the earth's magnetic field is 7,83 Hz. The Schumann resonance's effect on humans has been observed, among others, in experiments, where the so-called Faraday cage was created in the bunker. In the Faraday cage, the external electromagnetic field doesn't affect the interior of the cage. The mere isolating of the light on the outside of the bunker didn't have an effect on the test subjects' diurnal rhythm, but the isolation of the Schumann resonance did. When the Schumann resonance was artificially brought into the bunker, the test subjects' diurnal rhythm was restored. Some researchers call the Schumann resonance our planet's tuning fork and suggest that becoming exposed to this frequency causes natural healing. In addition to Schwartz, Simon, among others, has measured variations of the magnetic field the size of a milligauss, or oscillations, in the vicinity of Reiki healers.

In the context of energy healing, the effect of the Schumann resonance could be based on the synchronization of the energy healer's brain waves with the earth's magnetic field. Dr. Robert C. Beck researched several energy healers' brain wave activity with EEG as they were treating their patients. Irrespective of the method, the results were similar; all cases took place at the alpha level, with the frequency being 7,8-8,0 Hz on average. During the treatment, the healer's brain waves would seem to be in the same phase and the frequency synchronous with the earth's electromagnetic spectrum. In energy healing, one talks about acting as a channel, and of a connection to an outer source of energy: could the former be an indication of it?

Dr. Robert Becker and Dr. John Zimmerman also studied brain waves during energy healing, as well as the connection to the earth's magnetic field. They discovered that the healer's and the healee's brain waves were synchronized on an alpha level, which is typical of deep relaxation and meditation. In addition, they pulsated in the Schumann resonance, and also during these moments, the biomagnetic field measured from the healer's hands was at least 1000 times greater than usual. According to Zimmermann's hypothesis, the pivotal factor to explain energy healing is the Schumann frequency, about 7,8 Hz, which directs the healer's brain waves. He also suggests that the healer subconsciously adapts their speed of breath to the Schumann frequency, which helps the brain waves and the body's biofield to reach the Schumann frequency. The healee's brain waves become synchronized with the healer's brain waves. When the synchronizing occurs, the healer's hands will simultaneously emit energy. The energy emitted from the hands, the heat, could then be a sign of a connection being formed between the healee and the healer. Heat generation, or infrared signals has also been detected in measurements conducted during treatments. The heat and the sensation of heat are actually one of the most common observations in treatments.

What could be studied further

While reading about energy healing research and doing my own treatments, many thoughts have arisen about possible topics for further research. Out of interest in whether I could somehow bring out the effect of the treatments and make it more tangible, I also did some preliminary measurements of my own.

Thermal effect

The recurrent observation of both the healers and the healees is the sensation of heat. The heat can be felt even if the treatment is given from a little distance.

All bodies radiate heat. Heat radiation is electromagnetic radiation emitted from the body's surface. A physical body with about room temperature emits infrared radiation, whereas very hot bodies also emit a visible light. By measuring the heat radiation or with thermography, it has been possible in research to detect tumors, inflammations and other abnormal states of the body, sometimes even earlier than through other imaging techniques. Thermography is also a recognized method of diagnosis in medicine.

I did some preliminary measurements with the FLIR One thermal imaging camera, with 160 x 120 thermal resolution. The thermal imaging camera measures temperatures between -4°F and 248°F with the accuracy of 0,1°F. The thermal imaging camera takes a picture where the heat variation is displayed with color codes.

At first, I observed how the distribution of heat in my hands changed while giving a treatment. A clear change could be detected in the images at the start of a treatment. I did several repeated measurements, 10 in total. Each time, the distribution of heat in the palm would change so that the edge of the palm on the side of the little finger would immediately warm up when compared to the beginning of the treatment. In the images, the color changed from red to white, which is a sign of heating. Gradually the heat would spread over the whole palm, yet often focus in the center, which would stay warmer than the rest of the palm throughout the treatment. Also the tips of the fingers were warmer than the rest of the palm.

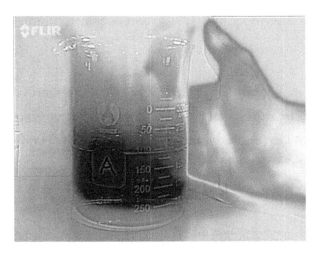

Fig. 10 s after the start of the treatment. The whiter the area, the warmer it is.

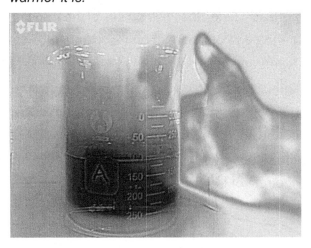

Fig. 20 s after the start of the treatment.

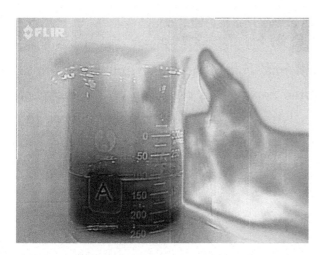

Fig. 30 s after the start of the treatment.

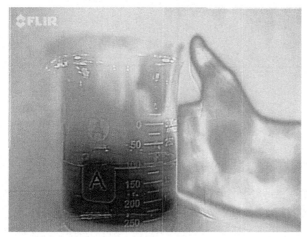

Fig. 60 s after the start of the treatment.

While giving a treatment, I might recognize the client's warmest body areas as being those that require the most treatment, are painful or are otherwise in need of healing. The heat seems to gradually even out to match the temperature of the surrounding tissue.

As I was eager to know what thermal imaging could reveal, I performed an initial study, examining my client's sore thumb with the thermal imaging camera. In the thermal image, the thumb could be seen as warmer than the rest of the hand at the beginning of the treatment. When I began the treatment, my hand turned immediately warmer than my client's hand. During the treatment, the heat in my own hand kept on growing by as much as a degree in the spot that I measured. My client's sore thumb warmed up by about two degrees in the course of a five -minute treatment.

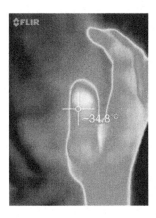

Fig. My client's hand at the beginning of the treatment. In the image, the sore thumb can be seen as being warmer (whiter the area, the warmer it is).

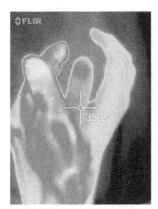

Fig. My hand on the left (reddish-yellow), the client's hand on the right (yellow, with red). My hand warms up while being treated.

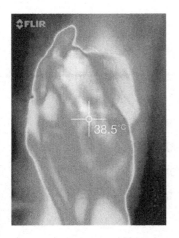

Fig. My hand warmed up by almost one degree in the measured spot.

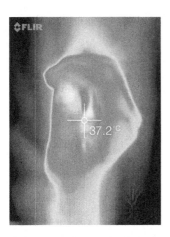

Fig. My client's hand after the treatment.

More detailed thermal imaging camera measurements could tell more about the effect of the energy healing. How does the heat distribution change during the healing? How does the heat change in the healer's hand? And how about the healee's hand? And how does the heat differ, if the healer just holds the hands still without healing? Does intuition regarding the areas to be healed correspond to the thermal imaging camera measurements? It would also be interesting to study, whether the heat is distributed in a similar way during treatments given by other energy healers.

Dr. Richard Pavek wanted to prove that energy healing is not just about the transfer of heat, and did experiments using several heat sensors. In the experiment, he found out first that the heat would rise higher in one of the healer's hands than in the other. A few minutes later, the patient's respiration rate decreased and they relaxed, and then the temperature of the patient's stomach area rose. Almost immediately after this, the temperature of the healer's other hand rose, too, by about a degree before it gradually dropped. The result is interesting; it is also said in Eastern traditions, e.g. in China and Japan that the area of the stomach is the center of well-being.

Ogawa et al., too, studied the temperature changes of the skin while two qigong masters healed volunteer patients. The skin temperatures rose for about 3-4 minutes during the treatment, by as much as 4°C. The rise of temperature can be a significant factor in energy healing, and this, too, ought to be studied further.

Water studies

Dr. Bernard Grad did many well-documented studies related to plants, water and healing. In the studies, the number of planted seeds, among others, was documented, as well as the height of the grown plants, their chlorophyll content and the quality of the leaves. Based on these, the researchers came to the conclusion that the seeds watered with treated water grew higher and healthier than those in the control group. The experiment was repeated and the results remained the same.

With infrared spectroscopy, Grad found changes in the molecular structures of the treated water: the number of hydrogen bonds between the water molecules decreased. In other studies, the treatment has been found to cause a change in the angle between the water molecules' atoms as well as in the surface tension.

I myself tried to measure the change in the surface tension of the water as a function of the treatment time with a capillary. The changes were, however, of the same magnitude as the accuracy of the measurement, so it was not possible to draw conclusions based on the results. A more accurate device would be needed to measure the surface tension.

Water sample (200 ml)	pH at the start (series 2 in brackets)	15 min after the treatment	30 min after the treatment	2 h after the treatment
Tap water	7,9 (7,7)	7,3 (7,5)	7,3 (7,4)	7,4 (7,4)
Filtered tap water	6,2 (6,3)	6,4 (6,4)	6,5 (6,6)	6,5 (6,6)
Bottled water	6,6 (6,7)	6,7 (6,8)	6,7 (6,8)	6,7 (6,8)

It would seem that energy healing helps create the best conditions for well-being. At least, this is what is indicated by many studies where the effect of energy treatments on the functioning of enzymes has been studied. Positively affecting enzymes would seem to function better, whereas negatively affecting would seem to fare worse. I decided to measure how an energy treatment affects the water's pH-value or acidity. According to the same logic, the pH should change toward the best pH for humans, which is said to be 7,30-7,45, which is also the pH of a human's saliva.

I measured the pH from tap water, filtered tap water and bottled water with a pH meter with a measurement accuracy of 0,1. At the start, the tap water's pH was the highest, 7,9. The filtered tap water's pH was lower than that of the bottled water, 6,2, with the bottled water's pH being 6,6. At first, I treated each for 15 minutes, measured the pH and treated for another 15 minutes. I also measured the pH a couple of hours after the end of my treatment. The tap water's pH dropped immediately to the level of 7,3, where it also stayed for the duration of the second round of treatment. The pH level of the filtered water, in

208

turn, rose slightly, just like the bottled water. The values didn't really change after the end of the treatment either. In my pH measurements, the pH thus seemed to approach a neutral level and also the best reading for humans. I did another series of measurements with almost the same results. These are, however, only two series of measurements, and it is not possible to draw conclusions yet based on them; further measurements are required.

EEG and what happens in the brain during healing

I did some preliminary EEG measurements with my Mindwave EEG headband. In the Mindwave EEG headband, there are only three electrodes, which it uses to measure the electroencephalogram, so it doesn't provide very accurate results compared to the EEG experiments used in hospitals, where electrodes are attached to the skin with the help of a cap. With the Mindwave EEG headband, one can gain a general view of the variation of the frequency and the voltage curve of the brain wave signal, as well as information on one's own level of concentration and relaxation. The frequency variation is divided into frequency areas: theta, alpha, beta, delta and gamma. Based on a few tests that I have made while giving energy healing, the values measuring both concentration and relaxation rise to the peak. The frequency areas stay equal at first, but when giving a longer treatment, the frequencies 0-10 Hz are emphasized. However, EEG measurements should be done for long periods of time before it is possible to draw more detailed conclusions from the above.

Effect on plants

The effect of energy healing on the speed of growth of plants has been observed in many studies, beginning with Grad's studies. Plants are easy to study, as it is easier to create almost identical research circumstances for them compared to animals and humans. As a try-out, I planted cress seeds in two jars, 16 seeds in each. Later, I noticed that jar B contained 17 seeds. I treated the water that I used to water jar A. At first, I treated the water for only 5 minutes, and for another few minutes in connection with each watering time. When 14 hours had elapsed from the time of planting, 15/16 seeds in jar A had split and were about to germinate. Of jar B's seeds, 12/17 had split. Jar A's 16th seed might have been a stone, which is why the table and graphs also show a corrected value.

When 38 hours had elapsed from the planting, 15/16 of jar A's seeds showed a small sprout and a little stem. Of jar B's seeds, all had sprouted and 14/17 showed already more sprout and stem. Of jar A's seeds, 4 were clearly more advanced than the other seeds in the same jar or the seeds in jar B.

Fig. 38 hours after the planting. The seeds watered with the treated water are in pot A and those watered with untreated water in pot B.

When 50 hours had passed since the planting, 15/16 seeds in jar A showed a small stem and leaves, compared to 13/17 of jar B's seeds. 62 hours after the planting, 13/16 sprouts in A had a 2-3 cm stem, and 10/17 in B. When 74 hours had passed since the planting, 15/16 had an over 3 cm stem in A, and 9/17 in B.

Fig. 74 hours after the planting.

The following table has been drawn to help perceive the differences between the jars watered with treated and untreated water. When comparing the values that I had chosen, the seeds watered with treated water, or series A, did better than the seeds watered with untreated water or group B. The values are comparable, but the development cannot be deduced from them, as I compared slightly different things at different measurement points, for instance at first the number of sprouted seeds, and later the number of plants of a certain height. All the values, however, described the growing of the plants. A (corrected) in the table refers to A's corrected value. In other words, in the calculations, the value used for the total number of seeds is 15, in case one non-sprouted seed was a stone.

In the column "Time (h)" is the time passed since the plantation, and in column "A" the results of jar A. In column "A (corrected)", the share of the non-sprouted seed has been deducted from the results. In column "B" are the results of jar B, and in the last column is a calculation of the % by which A's results were bigger compared to B's results.

Time (h)	A	A (corrected)	B	A vs. B (A corrected vs. B)
14	15/16=0,937	15/15=1	12/17= 0,705	33% (42%)
38	15/16=0,937	1	14/17= 0,823	14% (22%)
50	16/16=1	1	13/17= 0,764	31% (31%)
62	13/16=0,812	0,866	10/17= 0,588	38% (47%)
74	15/16=0,937	1	9/17= 0,529	77% (89%)
86	15/16=0,937	1	11/17= 0,647	45% (55%)

I also measured the plants' rate of growth, which wasn't very easy. I measured the height of each plant separately, and calculated their mean value. During the first 50 hours, the growth was almost identical, until at between 50-62 hours, the rate of growth of the plants in jar A grew faster than that of the plants in jar B, and at between 62-86 hours, even more so. The growth rate graph represents growth as a function of time.

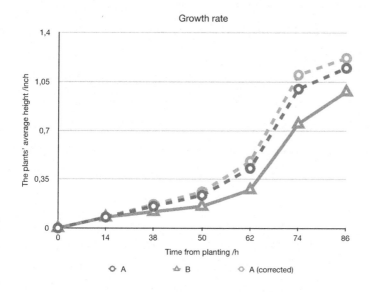

Growth rate

Time from planting /h

The plants' average height /inch

⊙ A   △ B   ⊙ A (corrected)

What we have here is yet another single measurement series, but the result is in line with the studies that Grad and others have carried out to determine the effect of energy healing on plants. Some studies on energy healing have discussed the dosage, among others: how much energy healing is needed at a time and is it even possible to determine the necessary dosage? It would actually be interesting to study whether it would affect the results if one would use water that had been treated even longer time. And are the results dependent on the particular healer? For instance, in studies, where the magnetic field variations were measured, the results rose to be manifold in the vicinity of experienced qigong masters compared to other energy healers.

Masaru Emoto's modified rice experiment

Can thoughts affect the end result, and do thoughts truly matter? I recommend trying out Masaru Emoto's rice experiment, which I mentioned already earlier in the Mind and matter –chapter. I performed a slightly modified version of the experiment myself.

I was about to throw a bowl of rice into the bin, when Masaru Emoto's rice experiment came to my mind. From a scientific point of view, one cannot draw any conclusions based on a single experiment that is not conducted in monitored circumstances. However, if millions of similar experiments are carried out with alike results, they can tell something statistically.

So what about if I put some already moldy rice in the jars? Would it still be possible to bring out the difference between these two jars? I put moldy rice from the same bowl into two jars, and drew a smiley face on the lid of one jar, with a heart on the side, and a sad face on the other jar's lid, with a lightning on the side. I placed the jars on the same cupboard in the kitchen, leaving the other jar on its own. I directed angry thoughts to the sad-faced jar, whereas I took the smiley-faced jar in my hand on a daily basis, and also gave it energy healing and thought positive thoughts about it.

Day 1: On the left, the jar with positive feelings, on the right, the jar with negative feelings.

Day 3.

Day 6.

Day 9.

Already on the third day, a difference could be seen between the jars. There was more mildew in the angry-faced jar, whereas the mildewing seemed to have stopped in the smiley-faced one. On the sixth day, the difference was even clearer. In addition to mildew, more moisture had formed in the angry-faced jar. In the smiley-faced jar, in addition to grey mildew, a whiter mildew seemed to be forming, like penicillin. On the ninth day, it looked as if the angry-faced jar contained twice the amount of mildew. After the ninth day, I lost my interest, and left the jars almost to themselves, although I might take the smiley-faced jar in my hand in passing and think positive thoughts for a moment. A week later, on the 16th day, a difference was still visible between the jars: at a glance, the angry-faced jar still contained about twice the amount of mildew.

When you carry out the experiment by yourself, the result will truly surprise. The result of a single experiment can obviously be a coincidence, although even then one could expect the most probable result to be that the jars look alike. It is especially surprising that the experiment has been carried out by millions of people over the years, and the results have been similar: Good fares better.

REFLECTIONS

CHAPTER 14. How to explain energy healing?

"My brain is only a receiver, in the Universe
there is a core from which we obtain knowledge, strength and
inspiration.
I have not penetrated into the secrets of this core,
but I know that it exists."
- Nicola Tesla

The more I do energy healing, the more I experience how difficult it is to put into words or to explain by means of current science, what energy healing is about. It is as if we would move to different world, to different dimensions. In the following chapter, however, I will try to compile together some of my observations, and what I think are the most essential points for developing in energy healing.

Information rather than energy

I don't like the term "energy healing", as it doesn't quite give the right idea. Many studies on remote healing, point, among others, to the fact that there is more to energy healing than the transfer of subtle energy through the healer's hands to the healee. "Energy" is also a misleading word, as it carries so many meanings. "Information" would do better to describe the forming of a connection and the transfer of information that occur in energy healing. Sure, the changes in the body felt by both the healer and the healee could be better described as "energy".

Information, too, could be thought of as energy. Also, "healing" is not the best possible word. It takes the attention to some external instance or source that heals and fixes the situation, although what really takes place is one's own inner work and observing, in other words, self-debate, connecting to oneself.

Connection is actually one of the most significant factors in energy healing. Dean Radin claims that *"mind/brain might be a self-observing quantum object, and as such, it resides within an entangled non-local medium"*. According to Radin's theory, all of our subconscious minds are in contact, entangled with each other all the time, but we may become aware of this connection only in special situations, such as in an emergency or in a moment of threat. Energy healers, however, may learn to be in this connected state during the healing so that their intention can help their healees.

If one seeks analogies for energy healing from other phenomena, light may well be the closest. I believe that energy healing cannot be described with just one model, but with several, just as the behavior of light is described with a dualistic model including both waves and particles. As with energy healing, heat is tightly bound to light. In the case of light, if the item is burning hot and the temperature above 1000°C, a large part of the radiation is already visible and is observed as light, such as in the case of light bulbs, a fire flame, and, of course, the Sun and other stars. And light, too, is about the transfer of information: it is used to transfer knowledge in optical fibers!

Quantum physics paved the way for a new way of thinking in science, and brought attention to the effect of the observer on observations. My efforts to understand my own experiences and energy healing have led to questions such as how we observe and view our world and reality, and how our mind and consciousness affect matter, our bodies, and healing. Energy healing leads to areas that science cannot provide an unambiguous answer to yet. One reason for this is the materialistic view of reality embraced by science, which doesn't consider mental processes. Yet the empirical observations that form the basis of knowledge occur on a mental level. The materialistic worldview is lacking in that it is unable to describe all perceived phenomena. The fact that the materialistic view is incapable of explaining all phenomena doesn't mean that it is wrong. The advent of quantum mechanics also didn't mean that Newton's physics was wrong, it just didn't work in all situations. If, however, we include in our worldview the information produced on a mental level, many things need to be reassessed. We can never obtain answers about independent reality, as observations always affect the measured information.

Classical deterministic physics leads to contradictions in the case of energy healing. If one assumes that the observations experienced during energy healing are real - whatever one means by "real" - these cannot be explained with the classical model of physics, because it doesn't take into account the mind. The healee's bodily sensations, the experience of flow in the body, even the physical changes and remote healing cannot be explained simply with energy flowing from the healer's hands. The hypothesis ought to include the effect of the thoughts, of the intention, and of other possible mental functions, in which case the energy emitted from the hands could be just a side product. Energy healing is one proof of there being a connection between the mind and the body. The research on energy healing can provide invaluable information, which can also help understand how mind works and our consciousness.

In the context of energy healing, Oriental cultures refer to energy bodies, which contain a different kind of information. The energy field of each human being is said to consist of five main layers, which interact with each other as follows:

1. **The physical energy body**. Our physical body is energy.
2. **The energy body or etheric energy body**. A side of the physical body maintaining health, which is often also referred to as the blueprint of the physical body.
3. **The emotional energy body, sometimes also called the astral body.** Keeper of our feelings.
4. **The mental energy body or thought body.** Keeps of our thoughts. Also our belief systems are stored here.
5. **The spiritual energy body, also causal body.** This is where our "consciousness" or the "higher self" resides.

Perhaps in energy healing, one affects the energy bodies rather than directly the physical body. This maybe the reason why it is difficult to measure the effect of energy healing from the physical body. A hypothesis on the mechanism of energy healing could be that energy healing affects the underlying mechanism regulating cells. Therefore it is perhaps not even possible to observe changes in the physical body or in the cells' function, at least not immediately.

The hypothesis of the energy bodies is also supported, among others, by the recent research by Wyde et al., which observed that the electromagnetic radiation of cell phones causes cancer especially among male rats. In the research, the rats were exposed to radiofrequency radiation at frequencies and modulations used in the US telecommunications industry, thus similar to the non-ionizing radiation of cell phones. Previously, the safety of cell phones, among others, have been defended by arguing that the low-energy electromagnetic radiation cannot bring about cell transformations and thus, is unable to cause cancer. Perhaps also the radiofrequency radiation confuses communication and affects the energy body, which can be seen as changes in the cell's function and as cancer tumors?

Energy bodies could also help explain electromagnetic hypersensitivity. Electromagnetic hypersensitivity refers to a state, where a person gets hypersensitive symptoms from electromagnetic radiation. Electromagnetic hypersensitivity is not really considered to be a "real" condition, even though the symptoms are real, because the link of the symptoms to the electromagnetic radiation has not been proved. In spite of their symptoms, the persons participating the experiments have not always been able to reliably state whether the electric field has been switched on or off in test situations. However, a change that occurs in the energy body is not necessarily directly visible as a change in the physical body.

The energy body model describes well what kind of information is linked to the different energy body layers. The deeper the level at which the changes occur in energy bodies, the more permanent these can be considered to be. One can think that in energy treatments one seeks to create a good connection between the different energy body layers so that the information can flow as smoothly as possible. Energy healing teaches quieting down and listening within. One's own inner experiences are the most important, as they broaden the perspective and bring the attention to that which is essential, and from which everything really originates. We possess within ourselves all the information and wisdom we need.

How is information transmitted?

How, then, is information transmitted in energy healing? A connection is formed between the healer and the healee, the healer and the source of energy, as well as the healee and the source, with the mediation of the healer.

My own understanding of energy healing is based on the flow of information. We exist constantly in different information fields. We are connected to some of them all the time, and we have the opportunity to become connected to others when we want. Sometimes the connection to essential fields can be broken or disrupted, and this is what energy healing aims to fix. Information flows on many levels.

Hypotheses regarding our connection to the surrounding field or the source of information have been made for years. The journalist Lynne McTaggart has collected several studies of this kind in her book, *The Field*. In addition to energy healing, the field model could serve to explain many other observed phenomena, which official science cannot explain at the moment, such as remote vision, telepathy and ESP, or extra sensory perception. In the model, everything is interconnected through the so-called zero point field.

The connection - whether one refers to the connection to the healee, the source or the field - is formed to one's own inner self. Different methods offer different techniques to establish the connection. The connection can be born right at the start of the treatment, or through quieting down. In addition, all healers form their own routine for creating the connection. This may include some of the following features: forming a meditative state, listening to one's own inner world, following or intentionally deepening one's breath, relaxing, visualizing or drawing energy healing symbols, using one's own mantras or the phrases one uses for starting the healing session, setting an intention or a wish for the treatment, and letting go of the wish. Often, for those who have given treatments for a longer period of time, starting a treatment can happen quickly, as the mind has already been trained to start the healing right away. It seems to help in creating the connection between the healer and the healee if the healer sets his or her hands on the spot to be treated. In remote healing, one can seek to form the connection through the name of the healee or photo or the like.

The most essential thing in starting the treatment and in forming the connection is that both the healer and the healee relax. When relaxing, the healer's conscious mind quiets down and all effort is left in the background. The healee, in turn, helps create the connection on a deeper level by relaxing. The forming of a connection between healer and healee can even involve, depending on the healer, various bodily sensations, such as the feeling of flow through the hands. I personally associate the birth of the connection with seeing colors behind closed eyes (often violet, and also undulating).

It is not necessary for the healee to try to relax or to aim for any particular state of being. However, relaxing is common, and it gets easier with further treatments, if there are difficulties the first time. The treatments can also induce "just" a light relaxation. Most commonly, the treatments involve a deep, dreamlike, meditative state, during which one is conscious of outer events, while still being turned inward. If the brain's activity and the level of consciousness is measured in a treatment situation with EEG or the electroencephalogram, the frequency will fall at the start of the treatment from the normal level of consciousness, or beta level (14-40 Hz) to alpha level (7,5-14 Hz). This corresponds to a state of relaxation that is common when the eyes are closed and one begins to visualize things or to meditate lightly. In energy treatments, relaxation can be so deep as to induce a state on the border of alpha and theta levels. At that state, the frequency is 7-8 Hz, which is the optimal area for visualization, affecting the mind and opening creative abilities. One is conscious of the limits of one's own body, while simultaneously being deeply relaxed. Theta-state (4-7,5 Hz) is often said to be a state where one experiences a spiritual connection and unity with all things and where one visualizes strongly and is exceptionally creative. The delta-state (0,5-4 Hz), in turn, is the state of deep sleep, which is dreamless and necessary, for instance, for healing. In addition to these, there is also the gamma-state (over 40 Hz), which is not very well known, but which is said to be involved with processing information and widening perspectives.

Energy healing is often described as a transition to a state where there is no time. Time loses its meaning and disappears. At the end of the treatment, it can be surprising to notice how much time has elapsed. The change of one's sense of time also suggests that the reality that we are dealing with is impossible to observe objectively. The physicist Paul Davies succeeds in describing time from the perspective of physics:

> "In the emerging picture of mankind in the universe, the future (if it exists) will surely entail discoveries about space and time which will open up whole new perspectives in the relationship between mankind, mind, and the universe... But what is now? There is no such thing in physics; it is not even clear that 'now' could ever be described, let alone explained, in terms of physics... Notions such as 'the past,' 'the present' and 'the future' seem to be more linguistic than physical... There is no universal now, but only a personal one—a 'here and now.' This strongly suggests that we look to the mind, rather than to the physical world, as the origin of the division of time into past, present, and future... There is none of this in physics... No physical experiment as ever been performed to detect the passage of time. As soon as the objective world of reality is considered, the passage of time disappears like a ghost into the night."

A quote from L. Dossey's article "How Healing Happens: Exploring the Nonlocal Gap"

Inner work

I have found the following things to be the most essential in my own energy healing work:

- **The state of consciousness changes and a connection is formed.** This is often related to relaxing or the deepening of breath. At the same time, the state is focused (as in a light hypnosis). The connection can be created in different ways.

- **A feeling of connection with the healee.** Once it has been formed, the sense of connectedness will remain in some way and will be easy to re-establish.

- **Listening within.** The sense of connection with an outer source of energy is born by listening to your inner sensations or inner world. The connection to the outer is, indeed, found through the connection within. The connection can also involve the experience of "oneness" and of an expanded consciousness.

- **Attitude.** Compassionate, loving, grateful. The ego gets out of the way of the treatment.

- **Letting go.** A pure wish stemming from the heart about the result: you set a goal, visualize it, and then let go of it. You don't actively attempt to give healing.

Listening to and observing your inner world and intuition will open the connection to healing. There is no need to try to do anything, treat or heal, not even to observe. Your own intuition will tell all that is needed. There is no need to "scan" through the body and search for spots to be treated. Often, the spots will feel different and hotter than the surrounding areas. The healer's inner work is essential for the treatment. This, too, ought not to be pursued separately, but instead the things to be dealt with will fall, so-to-speak, in front of the healer at just the right time, as it happened when I healed Melli.

The most visible part of energy treatments is the holding of the healer's hands over the spot to be healed or on the body, changing positions and spots from time to time. Both the healer and the healee do inner work. The channeling of the healer's energy also means listening to your own reactions, perhaps also visualizing how the energy flows in the healer's body and from there to the healee. Through visualizing, you simultaneously train the body to heal. The healee does not need to do anything, but they may have feelings or even physical reactions, which help relax and stabilize the mind. It is said that the healee's energy body is stabilized.

Often in connection with complementary treatments, there is talk of the effect of both the healer's and the healee's faith in the treatment. An energy treatment works through a mind-body connection, activating the body's natural ability to heal itself. Whether you believe in the effect of the treatment has no importance. The treatment will affect the healee in exactly the same way whether they believe in its effect or not. As a matter of fact, even the healers don't need to believe in the effectiveness of the treatment. Evidence of this can be found, for instance, in Bengston's research, in which the most skeptical persons were selected to give healing, and the mice would still heal. My own view is that the healers' trust in what they do will strengthen the treatment. The work takes place from the heart, from within connectedness, not from the ego.

It is said that every thought is energy, too. You can affect things with thoughts; these can lead to change or to the start of a new process. In the 1970s, the slogan "Your thoughts create your reality" became famous, and at the time, people tried to manifest a fancy car or house. However, you cannot direct things with your ego. The quantum physicist Amit Goswami explains this by saying that in quantum physics, objects are probability waves, out of which consciousness selects the one that will be realized. Our consciousness, in other words we ourselves, can choose our own reality. We choose our own reality, but we don't choose with the ego, but rather from a deep level of common consciousness where we are all one. On a mental level, our own values guide us, and if we act from such fundamental values as love, justice, truth and goodness, the situation will change. Instead of focusing on matter, we bring our focus to these values, through which we can act and influence. Then we exist in a state where we are all one and there are no conflicts, as the same consciousness affects everything. We cannot direct things through our own, separate ego. Manifestation occurs through oneness.

Anybody can learn to give energy healing. It is a skill that we have been endowed with already at birth, but that many have unlearned as other skills have developed and our worldview has formed. It is about observing and reacting to observations, breaking customary models and reappraisal. I hope that my book will help try it out, so that everyone can form their own opinion. Energy healing is so-called "slow living", which there is much talk about these days, so one experiment will not tell all. However, sometimes even one treatment will bring about change. It is worth listening to the healer's instructions, on, for instance, how many treatments they recommend, because, as I have said already, the treatments are personal, and often specific to individual healers. It is also not recommended to try out different treatments in combination, but rather to have one series of treatments at a time with one healer.

I, too, often give a recommendation to my healee on the first treatment. The recommendation depends on what they are looking for from the treatment. It is not the energy healer's task to intervene with diagnoses or medical care, rather I aim to help within the boundaries that the healee expresses about a given situation. Energy healing is never harmful, and it can be given at all times.

Although energy healing doesn't have a goal – in the same way that many other forms of treatment do – the healer's and the healee's observations, and especially the healee's reactions to the treatment influence the effect of the healing. It is not necessary to say anything during a treatment, not even a word, and yet the treatment can be a very powerful experience for the healee, and often for the healer, too.

When treating and relaxing, the healee's conscious mind quiets down. It is said that our conscious mind can process just a fraction of the information that our unconscious, subconscious mind can. When the conscious mind quiets down, the unconscious mind starts working more freely and producing images, bringing forth memories and feelings. In hypnosis, this is used more actively as a tool, and with guidance, you can help, for instance, unravel unwanted patterns of behavior. In energy treatments, often after the first phase, which is the good relaxation, even surprising memories, feelings and associations can come to the healee's mind. Facing these can be just what the healee need. Sometimes also images experienced by the healer during a treatment can help the healee realize something essential that may stand in the way of healing.

CHAPTER 15. Facing inner wisdom

Nothing in life is to be feared,
it is only to be understood.
Now is the time to understand more,
so that we may fear less.
- Marie Curie, physicist and chemist (1867-1934)

I believe that a new perspective on life revealed itself to me when I became opened to such a possibility. As I follow this new path, I constantly encounter new challenges, which, little by little, expand my understanding of life and enable access to my inner wisdom.

Self-reflection

What happened after Melli's case, and the experiences of energy healing that I have described in this book? I have encountered many exciting new experiences of energy healing and I still do. I decided to stay on the path that I stepped onto when I went to the Reiki course on that one November evening, and it has indeed been interesting.

For me, energy healing has been about questioning my own beliefs and about breaking boundaries. It is said that the more rationally you think, the more work you need to do with your ego. You need to melt the shell that is around you. If you already have a firm foundation in life, you will not easily start breaking it down. There is no reason to do that. Beginning to question your beliefs may require facing a personal crisis, after which you are more willing to look at things from a different viewpoint. What you learn is always reflected up against the starting point and knowledge that you have already internalized. The steeper the walls are that you have erected, the longer it will take to break them down.

Every healing session, whether doing self-healing or giving energy healing to others, has simultaneously been a lesson to myself: what does energy healing awake in me? While treating Melli, I gained the insight that I MYSELF am not what does the healing or can affect its result. I am just a channel, and I can only express a wish and then let go of it. All possible futures or probabilities for various events exist and with my thoughts and attention, I guide toward a given option. I have experienced very strongly how something from the outside, perhaps from our unified consciousness, influences the healing.

Learning something new often follows a linear learning curve, except in the case of possible setbacks. When learning and getting familiar with the energy healing, the learning process cannot be said to occur in a linear manner. "Stairs" would serve better to describe the process. At times you get an insight, which lifts the energy, you could say, to a whole new level. Climbing the stairs is also a personal thing. You can never know in advance what you need to realize in order to develop. Therefore when training energy healing, things are not fed to the students ready made, instead the teacher will only point in the direction where you can search for answers. You may already be giving up, thinking that "this wasn't my thing", when you suddenly may experience something special. You may notice, for example, while giving healing, that you can feel a flow through your hands and body. Or you may simply realize that you can sense in you mind where it is that your client needs healing. Or then else, you may start seeing colors during the healing, or feel that you and your client's body contours disappear and that you are one and the same... For those used to systematic planning and living by the clock, energy healing can be a challenge. However, they can become your resource that can totally revolutionize your life, as it happened to me.

The most significant personal insights that I have gained through energy healing have had to do with my own role and purpose. I have come to realize that it is me who decides over my own life and also affects the end result. It is pointless to blame others. It is I myself who has created all the obstacles and boundaries in my own mind, and I myself can also unravel them. I can also affect the end result with my own thoughts and attitude. This insight has been empowering; it has affected my own well-being, goals, and daily life in general. I myself am responsible for everything, including my own well-being and health. I can do anything if I really want to!

The mind plays a significant role, among others, in manifesting, energy treatments, and healing. Therefore, I became interested in hypnosis, which also involves working with the mind and consciousness. I trained to become a hypnosis practitioner in order to better understand the phenomenon. Just like with energy healing, there are many misunderstandings related to hypnosis. My experiences of hypnosis are the subject of another book, but getting to know hypnosis has also helped me gain a better understanding of energy healing. Also, energy healing has similar characteristics as hypnosis. Hypnosis can be described as an altered state of consciousness, where deep physical and psychological relaxation takes place. In hypnosis, the normal waking consciousness drops to an alpha state, or the state that immediately precedes falling asleep. It is the same state as when the mind is creative. It is easy to visualize, to get ideas and thoughts, and memories one has forgotten come to mind more easily. Similarly, energy healing and hypnosis are phenomena that are experienced with your senses, and come to your awareness, and these can be experienced as your own subjective experiences. They can be observed, and studied. As in hypnosis, in energy healing, too, the field of perception is narrowed down when relaxing. Awareness of your surroundings becomes gradually meaningless, and is left outside conscious perception. Attention becomes focused on the inner world. The feeling is relaxed and simultaneously focused. In energy healing, the healer will not often guide the healee. Instead, the healee's attention can move freely in the pace of their own imagination and thoughts.

During my life, in the context of different projects, I have done a lot of cross-disciplinary work involving a dialogue between various disciplines. While working on my doctoral thesis, I noticed that even such very closely related disciplines as chemistry, information technology, and physics could have difficulties conversing between them. Once a common language has been found, you can, however, reach a level that none of these could reach on their own. Even though energy medicine is not yet an official discipline, my own understanding of energy healing has been significantly helped by seeking answers in the direction of hypnosis and science.

Energy healing has taught me to "look at" myself from further away. Gradually during self-healing, I began to see a connection between what I have done previously, what I do now, and what I believe I should do. It just started feeling increasingly clear and natural, how everything is related. Gradually I also started adding to my wish list, which I update regularly, images of giving energy healing in a homey treatment room by the sea, training or giving a lecture on well-being, writing a book with a cat sitting next to me... I also began to create a business plan, and dreamt of what I could do for a living and how I could best help others, too. I never actually made a decision to leave my permanent job; it just felt natural and inevitable that it had to go. And I haven't regretted it, because I made my choice from the heart, based on the values that I want to live by.

Energy healing entails a change in your way of thinking. It is self-debate and leads to inner growth, which will affect your entire life and close relations. Well-being comes as a by-product. Nowadays, I would describe energy healing as the forming of a new kind of connection to your inner self and inner wisdom.

Inner wisdom also of help to science

Inner wisdom refers to direct knowing or subjective understanding. There are a growing number of instances that share experiences and do research on inner wisdom (also referred to as noetic sciences) around the world. One of the largest of them is the Institute of Noetic Sciences (IONS) in the US, which was founded in 1973 by one of the first astronauts, Edgar Mitchell, out of the wish to gain better understanding of his own space flight experiences. On his return to

Earth after his moonwalk, Mitchell had a revolutionary experience that changed the former rational and physical worldview of the engineer. He had a deep sensation of how the blue globe, onto which he was returning, was part of a living, harmonious whole, and that we people were part of it, too. Mitchell referred to this as "the universe of consciousness" and realized how little we actually understand. IONS currently hosts 220 discussion groups in 50 countries, providing support for both personal and collective growth.

We use inner wisdom often unawares, when innovating and making decisions, among others. Also, in the history of science, there are many cases, where scholars have used inner wisdom, that is intuition, dreams, or otherwise the unconscious mind, or had premonitions or visions about solving a problem.

The Russian chemist Dmitri Mendelejev had a dream about a table in which all the chemical elements occupied their own specific places based on their atomic and chemical properties. The dream helped Mendelejev to form the periodic table of elements, which he drew on a piece of paper as he woke up. Likewise, Niels Bohr drew the model known as the Bohr's atomic model after having had a dream one night where electrons revolved around the atom's nucleus just like planets circle the Sun. Bohr's atomic model is still taught in schools today. The German chemist Friedrich Kekulé von Stradonitz invented the benzene molecule ring and thereby the structure of aromatic compounds with the help of intuitive visions, and "dreaming". He discovered the ring shape after having had a daydream of six snakes seizing each other's tails until they joined in a ring connecting each other from head to tail.

He figured out that six carbon atoms of benzene could also form a stable configuration that way. Kekulé developed further the theory of chemical structure following similar methods. René Descartes also had visions, and he described how the divine spirit told him about a new philosophy that combined mathematics and philosophy into analytic geometry.

Dreams had an important effect on Albert Einstein's inventions, too. When he was young, he had a dream that he described as follows (quotes from Einstein's book *On Cosmic Religion and Other Opinions and Aphorisms,* A. Webb's article "Six Times Dreams and Mysticism Changed the Course of Science"):

"*I was sledding with my friends at night. I started to slide down the hill but my sled started going faster and faster. I was going so fast that I realized I was approaching the speed of light. I looked up at that point and I saw the stars. They were being refracted into colors I had never seen before. I was filled with a sense of awe. I understood in some way that I was looking at the most important meaning in my life.*"

The dream acted as a basis and inspiration for the theory of relativity. Einstein said that his scientific career was like meditating in this dream. Einstein is told to have said:

"*The intuitive mind is a sacred gift and the rational mind is a faithful servant. We have created a society that honors the servant and has forgotten the gift.*"

He is also told to have said:

"I believe in intuition and inspiration. Imagination is more important than knowledge. For knowledge is limited, whereas imagination embraces the entire world, stimulating progress, giving birth to evolution. It is, strictly speaking, a real factor in scientific research."

When you work closely on a certain topic, whether it is a research problem or something else, all information and perceptions are absorbed by the conscious mind. While asleep or relaxing, the data becomes organized in a new way in the mind. The subconscious mind processes, organizes and modifies the information received, and a clearer and more holistic understanding of the issue is generated. Often, when there is a strong emotional bond to a certain issue, intuition seems also to work more eagerly.

In science, too, both rational and intuitive thinking are used all the time, although this type of cognitive processing is not a scientific method as such. The mind requires sleep, intuition and subconscious processing to resolve a problem and to produce innovative ideas. Because inner wisdom is used anyway, couldn't it be used more systematically, focusing on the development of inner wisdom?

In science, it would be well worth trying to produce knowledge through methods that don't use rational thinking, such as dream viewing, clair or psychic senses like clairvoyance, remote viewing, mediumship, channeling information, out-of-body exercises, past lives, and generally by developing intuitive skills. What these have in common is having

239

direct access to information, and knowing without "normal" senses, logical thinking or memory. The methods differ a lot in terms of their accuracy, way of learning, reliability, accessibility and possibility to control. A common feature between them all is a different way of accessing information, through direct or inner wisdom, with intuition playing a significant role. Perhaps one day, relaxing and meditation are taught as methods of conducting science, and sufficient sleep is emphasized. To quote Henri Poincaré (from his book *Science and Method*): *"It is by science that we prove, but by intuition that we discover."*

There is an increasing amount of anomalies, observations and experimental results that don't fit the current scientific model. In many of them, the mind, which has been ignored in science for a long time, plays an important role. The amount of observations is such that these kinds of experiences cannot be dismissed. Professor Edward Kelly et al., among others, have compiled cases that don't fit the strongly dualistic model of the mind and brain in the book *Irreducible mind: Towards a psychology for the 21st century*. In the book they suggest that we should reject the current, dominant materialistic approach and bring the mind and consciousness back to their place, as an important part of science.

In order for the methods of inner wisdom or direct knowing to become accepted methods for doing science, these would presumably require clearer and more systematic definition. Naturally, such specification is not unambiguous, and perhaps not even possible. Accessibility is another matter: methods are needed that can help access knowledge.

Energy healing provides one way to access inner wisdom, and it can be learned by anyone.

At first, the above may seem impossible. However, as far as I can see, research world doesn't have another alternative. The direction of research is always influenced by the scholars' approach, and especially by their worldview. If the possibility of the existence of the spiritual phenomena is ignored, this will inevitably lead to research and methods that exclude something essential. Using the language of quantum mechanics: if you want to observe particles, you will find particles. Dr. Tarja Kallio-Tamminen tells an example of this in her book Kvanttilainen todellisuus, in English Quantum reality. It is said that in the Western countries, astronomers began to perceive changes in the sky only after Copernicus' observations. Until then, the world beyond the moon was assumed to be static. In China, instead, astronomers had made observations about new stars and solar flares already hundreds of years earlier.

Energy healing as a means to access inner wisdom

A human being is more than a physical entity. There are research results supporting the notion that thoughts matter and affect also healing. Placebo is a well-known phenomenon, and it is used in Western medicine. However, the reason why placebo can heal is not understood. Science is not able to explain how the mind and thoughts can have such an effect as that the body's well-being will increase and the person will heal. The human being is still one of the biggest mysteries for us. Roughly speaking, in medicine, a human being, healing and also placebo are dealt with according to Newton's model of classical physics. Humans are perceived as biological machines, and the mind and consciousness aren't seen as having an effect on the physical world.

However, in medicine, there are still claims that the proof is inadequate for us to say that the incurably ill can heal through positive thinking. As long as science is unable to create a model for how the mind works when a person heals, it is not to be expected that medicine will change its position. The influence of positive thinking is, however, undeniable: it affects the patient's frame of mind and makes them feel better. We all have the option to choose the way we relate to our lives and challenges. According to research, when experiencing negative feelings such as anxiety and depression, self-centeredness becomes more accentuated. It is hard to see beyond oneself, to perceive the larger picture or positive things in the surroundings. Dr. Emma Seppälä states in her book *The Happiness Track*, that when we experience positive feelings, it is easier for us to see further and to plan the future, form relationships with, and also seek support from others. It seems as if positive thinking would open a channel that frees from self-centeredness and creates a connection to the rest of the world.

Energy healing can offer a tool for positive thinking and for accessing inner wisdom. It can help realize that which is most important, while the unessential issues diminish, recede and loose their importance. My opinion is that you need to personally experience energy healing before you are able to say anything about it. The following exercise is a taster of energy healing, if you are willing to give it a try.

For this exercise, find a place to be a moment on your own. Find a good position and take a deep breath in and a deep breath out. When reading these words, wherever you are, I am sending you remote healing. If you like, pay attention to your bodily sensations, your thoughts or your emotions passing by. You can set your hands on your face, either at a few inches in the air or right on the forehead or cheeks. After a moment, move them to your chest, and then to the stomach. Alternatively, you can just hold your hands where you feel you need the most energy at this very moment. Otherwise you can just be, let the breath move in and out its own, natural way, and just listen to your sensations. If you like, you can close your eyes for a moment and then continue reading.

When you continue reading again, notice how you feel. It is not necessary to feel or experience anything special. If you feel the need to somehow vent your experience, then write it down right now, without any particular censorship or analysis. Just let the words flow, or draw a picture, whichever feels the best.

CHAPTER 16. Concluding remarks

*"The force is an energy field
created by all living things,
it surrounds us, it penetrates us,
it binds the galaxy together."*
- Obi-Wan Kenobi in Star Wars

In this book, I have wanted to share my own experiences of energy healing and what I have learned and realized during the process. Getting to know energy healing has been a journey of exploration for me, a journey that is still continuing. There is still a lot to study, to learn and to gain a better understanding of.

It has been my intention to invite you to reflect on your own ways of thinking. Perhaps your current way of thinking is not the only right one, and it would be worthwhile trying to break boundaries. In the book, I have described science and several studies that tell their own story about how our consciousness affects the reality that we observe, and how our mind affects our body, among other things.

In the course of my journey, I have come to realize a few things, some of which I will present in the following. I hope that they, in turn, will give rise to insights in others.

From objectivity to subjectivity

Even though research results are important, I like to emphasize personal experience. Perceptions and experiences are always subjective: what works for one person may not necessarily work for another. Therefore, be open to new things, and dare to challenge. Experiment, and don't reject until you have formed your own opinion. The unquestionable advantage of energy healing is that it doesn't have harmful side effects. Each one of us has to find our own answers and arguments in life, and not even scientific research can always provide sufficient proof for all.

From materialism to idealism

Writing this book has been a process that is related to the issues that I faced already as a first-year physics student, attending Emeritus Professor of Theoretical Physics K.V. Laurikainen's Philosophy of Science course. At the time, I had no idea how unique that course was. While physics students graduate as masters and doctors of philosophy, philosophy actually has very little to do with the physics that is currently being taught. Naturally, philosophy is taught in different faculties. The materialistic view has increasingly taken over the teaching of physics, and I agree with professor Laurikainen's view of the early 1990s, that more cross-disciplinary studies are required, nowadays even more than then. If the perspective is limited to just a particular viewpoint and if, for instance, the possibility of spiritual phenomena is bypassed, it will inevitably lead to research and methods that leave out something essential.

From separation to unity

Research confirms that the distance doesn't matter: the healee can be at a distance from the healer. According to quantum physics, this is possible, and time is also irrelevant. Quantum physics teaches that a

245

photon can be located in two different places at the same time. Actually, a photon is located everywhere before it is observed. A photon can also be a wave or a particle, depending on the observer's expectations and measurement system. Space and time are relative observations rather than absolute measurements. All protons are interlinked through the universe. Experiments have shown that when we influence one proton, we simultaneously influence all the protons that are linked to it elsewhere in the universe. Quantum physics allows the thought of an expanded world, where we aren't just bound to the Earth, but are all connected to each other in the universe. We are all one, all part of a collective consciousness, and all fundamentally part of the same energy.

From medicine to complementary treatments

In the Oriental tradition, the approach to health is often focused on the prevention of illness: harmony and balance are sought, followed by health and well-being. Roughly speaking, in the East, health is approached trough the mind, whereas in the West, it is approached though matter and body. The center of everything, however, is the human being, whose well-being is the most important issue. Therefore, we ought to find the best way to combine both approaches, in other words, to combine Western medicine and Oriental teachings on Integral Medicine.

In Finland, energy healing is not included yet in the public health care system, but in some countries, it is. In the US, energy treatments are widely in use, for instance in hospitals, where they are offered as a support before and after operations. Also, they are used for pain relief, stress and recovering from surgeries. They are also used to relieve the side effects of cancer treatments. According to the American Hospital Association, currently about 60% of American hospitals offer Reiki in hospitals' services. In England, energy healing is widely used in hospitals, mostly through volunteer services. Some hospitals have also hired energy healers on permanent contracts.

The future direction in Western healthcare is probably some form of integrative medicine. It will combine Western medicine with methods from other healing wisdom traditions. The aim is to help prevent illnesses and to increase holistic health care. In addition to treating the human being, integrative medicine also aims to provide tools (including meditation, visualization exercises, creative self-expression, self hypnosis, and energy healing), whereby you can affect your own well-being. The aim is to help people to be active and take responsibility comprehensively for their own well-being.

From illusions to reality

In this book, there are research results on the effect of the mind on, among others, random number generators, and even healing. Thoughts and attitude do matter. Energy healing has helped me see the world in a new way. What I do, and even think, always matters. When I live my life according to values that I myself can accept, I am in balance. I will deal with issues that I face immediately from within unity and common consciousness, where my values also stem from. From there, I can also manifest the forthcoming.

From analysis to intuition

This has been my most liberating insight. Previously, I had learned to analyze everything that I experienced in my life - everything that I saw, felt, heard, smelled and tasted. Besides my own senses, I had learned to use measuring and all kinds of measuring devices, from sensors to supercomputers. I had learned to base my decisions on the results of my analysis.

I feel that by starting to use my intuition and the tools of my mind, I have freed myself from analysis. Analyzing belongs to the materialistic world, whereas intuition doesn't. My conclusion is that understanding ourselves and learning to use our inner wisdom – intuition – is the key to all the information that we need. I have everything that I need: I am my own guru.

From quantum physics to energy healing

My journey has gone from the realm of science and rational thinking to spirituality and inner wisdom. On many nights at the time of writing this, in my dreams, I have met my physics teachers from school and University, including the late emeritus professor K.V. Laurikainen. In a dream, he told me that he supported me, and that a cross-disciplinary approach and an opening of perspectives are indeed needed. Therefore I can only challenge you to start off on your own expedition.

CHAPTER 17. Frequently asked questions about energy healing

I am often asked to describe, for instance during my courses, how to explain energy healing shortly for those who aren't familiar with it. What would you say to your own doctor, for example, if you wanted to let them know that you use energy healing? Or as a healer to your own clients? Often there is a difficulty in finding the right, appropriate concepts. Here then, are my answers to some of the most frequently asked questions about energy healing.

What is Reiki? What is energy healing?

Reiki is originally a Japanese method of natural healing. It can be used to relax, to improve well-being, to relieve pain and to support healing, among others. A Reiki treatment strengthens the body's own immune system and natural healing processes. The healer channels "universal life energy" into the healee (chi, prana, etc., cf. acupuncture, in which one also affects the flow of chi).

Energy healing is about focusing on the cause behind the symptoms. Instead of directing the focus and energy to the ailment and symptoms, such as a headache, the focus is brought deeper, to the cause from which the headache results. The underlying cause is examined from the viewpoint of energy. The body's symptoms don't show up out of coincidence. If one is able to identify the cause, it can also be changed. Energy healing is about inducing a subtle change of direction.

What is "universal life energy"?

Universal life energy is called by many different names depending on the culture (chi, prana, etc.). In more scientific contexts one speaks of subtle energy. The energy being referred to is not the same kind of energy as what is usually meant by energy in Western countries and in physics. One can speak of immaterial energy at the level of the mind or information. In connection with energy healing, one sometimes also speaks of high- or low-vibrating energy, which cannot be explained by the materialistic worldview or studied with the current methods. This energy could best be described as a vibration occurring at the level of the mind.

How does quantum physics support energy healing?

Quantum physics explains the behavior of our world and our reality at the subatomic level. It is the fundamental explanation behind all our experiences, including energy healing. According to quantum physics, all the possibilities for our experiences exist at the subatomic level. Our observations also affect what we experience.

Quantum physics also includes the idea that deep down we are all vibrating energy. At the subatomic level, it is impossible to draw the line where one of us ends and another begins. Thus we are all one. According to quantum physics, particles can also affect each other from a distance, that is entanglement. It doesn't directly follow from this, yet, that remote healing works, but similar ideas underlie both. Also, according to quantum physics, place and time are irrelevant.

How does energy healing work?

Energy healing cannot be explained from a materialistic worldview, which treats the mind as a product of the brain. The "energy" in energy healing is not the same as the energy dealt with in physics. Energy healing is actually one indication of the fact that the materialistic worldview is incapable of explaining all perceived phenomena. When we expand our worldview to encompass the idea that it is the mind that creates our reality, including our material world, energy healing becomes more understandable, too.

Consciousness could be the source energy or creator energy that Reiki refers to. Consciousness is an all-encompassing, omnipresent web, which we are connected to at all times. Sometimes the connection can be blocked for various reasons and we become isolated. Another person, like a healer, can help us re-establish our connection to the web and to the flow of pure consciousness.

Do all energy healers actually do Reiki?

All energy healers channel universal life energy, but not all of them do Reiki. It is only possible for the healers who have received Reiki initiations to give Reiki healing. Sometimes those who have had a Reiki treatment have an intensified feeling of energy flowing through their hands. It is said that the Reiki channels can open by themselves during treatments. In his articles, Bengston mentioned the possible connection between the teacher and the student, and suggested that a mere connection with the teacher could suffice to transfer the ability to heal. Perhaps in Reiki, the simple connection to the founder of Reiki, Mikao Usui, suffices, as established via the teachers.

251

How do you learn energy healing?

The easiest and most common way to learn energy healing is by attending a course. Energy healing is, however, only learned by doing, in other words by giving treatments to yourself and others. Having energy treatments also supports the learning process. It is also said that the ability to heal is there at birth; in the courses, the old skill is simply brought back to action. Reiki is almost always learned in courses.

Why are initiations done in Reiki?

Initiations are part of the Reiki method and Reiki's way to open the connection to the Reiki healing awareness. The initiation opens the mind to function as a channel and to connect with the joint knowledge, which could be referred to as the *higher consciousness* or *Reiki's source energy.*

Are the symbols required for doing Reiki? Must they always be drawn?

The symbols are "keys" that allow to access Reiki knowledge and help in learning to do Reiki healing. Reiki can be done in many ways. In my own courses, I teach to work with the symbols particularly at the beginning, so as to create a personal, interactive relationship to the symbols and to what they induce in yourself and the mind. You learn to heal with the help of the symbols. However, they are not necessary for Reiki to work. When the interaction is there, I personally don't always feel the need to draw the symbols. My own intuition and heart will tell what is required. You can draw the symbols whenever needed, or you can teach yourself to draw them every time at the start of a treatment.

What is remote healing? How does it work?

In remote healing, a treatment is sent to a healee from a distance. The healee can be even on the other side of the globe. In quantum mechanics, it has been shown that you can affect particles from a distance, even from thousands of miles away. Time and distance are irrelevant.

Does one need to take a break from healing if there is grief, illness or challenges in the healer's life?

It is certainly good to focus on self-healing first. Grief, illness and heavy life events take their toll, and energy healing will help cope with the experiences and give strength to pursue daily life. However, there is no need to take a break from healing others; after all, you receive healing yourself while healing others. Here, too, it is worth listening to your own intuition. Naturally, you can help others best when you also take care of yourself and your own well-being.

What does research say about energy healing?

There are only a few studies of a high enough quality and sufficient breadth on energy healing to-date, but it is already possible to state that energy healing relaxes the body, relieves pain in different acute and chronic pains, lifts spirits and relieves anxiety. The relaxing effect of energy healing has been shown in measurements, for instance in the form of a healthier heartbeat and blood pressure. It is challenging to research energy healing, due to variables related to the phenomenon that we don't necessarily know yet, let alone are able to measure with the current methods.

What can energy healing be applied to?

Energy healing is a good tool for self-healing: it helps to relax and to lift spirits. It can be used like meditation. For instance, you can do bodily meditation, where you do self-healing, using the hand positions of Annex 1 while meditating. Or you can combine meditation with remote healing, and send to yourself remote healing while meditating.

You can also treat others with energy healing. Energy healing can be used as a first aid for any ailment. It can be used for recent ailments that have developed over a short period of time, such as a headache, any kind of pain, wounds, or sprains. It can also be used to support the healing of ailments that have developed over a longer period of time. There are no restrictions as to when it can be used. It has not been found to have side effects. You can always give Reiki, even in a situation where a decision has been made to stop all other, Western treatments.

What can energy healing NOT be applied to?

Energy healing can always be used. There are no restrictions. Because it can be given even without touching and from a distance, it can also be used to heal clients from a distance, or when the spot to be healed cannot be touched. Energy healing can also be used to treat animals, including dangerous animals, with remote healing.

Glossary

Absorption - The act of being retained or soaked into something. The opposite of absorption is emission.

Amplitude - The maximum extent of a vibration deviating from the position of equilibrium

Atom - Originates from the Greek word *atomos* – undivided. The smallest component of a chemical element, consisting of a nucleus and surrounding electrons.

Aura - A glowing, imprecise subtle "energy field" surrounding objects, humans and animals, which some people are able to feel or to see. Changes in the aura are thought be caused by changes in the chakras.

Biofield - A field devoid of mass, not necessarily electromagnetic, which surrounds living systems. Possibly related to the aura.

Biopsy - Taking a sample or a cell specimen from a living body.

Causality - The relation between a cause and its effect.

Chakra - According to some Eastern traditions or disciplines, a nonphysical energy or power center in the human energy body. Chakras are thought of as energy- or information channels, or portals, to a human body.

Chi (qi) - Universal life energy in Chinese culture.

Clinical trial - A medical or experimental trial conducted to prove, for instance, the effectiveness and safety of a medication or treatment.

Dao (Tao) - Chinese for way or path, a fundamental concept of Taoism.

Determinism - A philosophical view, according to which all events have specific causes, and different outcomes would not be possible.

Double-blind experiment - The information about the experiment, i.e. what kind of treatment is given to the healee, is kept from both the healer and the healee in order to exclude placebo effect.

Dualism - A dual concept of reality, usually between (spirit) mind and matter. (ref. Descartes.)

Ego - The conscious mind, a part of identity that is thought of as the self, or I.

Electron - A particle that rotates around the nucleus of an atom. The electron is negatively charged.

Emit - To send. The opposite of emitting is absorbing.

Empirical - Based on observation or on experience.

Hypothesis - A proposed explanation for a phenomenon based on a theory.

Intensity - Quantity that describes energy transfer, power per unit area.

Ki - Universal life energy in Japan.

Mana - Universal life energy in Hawaii.

Metaphysical - (in Greek, *meta* means "after", in other words, "after physics"). A subfield of philosophy that deals with reality and the essence of existence in general. Ontology belongs to metaphysics.

Nocebo - Negative expectations affect the result of a treatment, or health, in a negative way.

Non-local - Phenomena that does not vary with distance. Non-local interaction can be faster than the speed of light.

Null hypothesis - A typical test result that can be expected from the outset.

Ontology - The fundamental nature of being; a view of the nature of reality.

Placebo - Healing without treatment containing a medical substance.

Pneuma - Universal life energy in Greece.

Prana - Universal life energy in India.

Qi - See chi.

Qigong (chi kung) - A Chinese practice which is used to increase the flow of universal life energy.

Remission - The easing of disease in a chronic illness.

Resonance - "Synchronous vibration", occurs when an external oscillating force increases a system's vibration at it's natural frequency.

Schumann Resonance - The Earth's resonance phenomenon of electromagnetic radiation (generated, e.g. by lightning), occurring at a frequency of approximately 7.83 Hz.

Subtle body - A non-physical part of the body that maintains the physical body's health and well-being, according to some traditions.

Teleology - A philosophical approach, in which the existence of a phenomenon is explained by referring to its purpose, result or goal.

Type II error - A wrong conclusion that occurs when a statistical test confirms a false null hypothesis.

Usui Shiki Ryoho - Usui's natural system of healing founded by and named after Mikao Usui.

References

The Bengston Energy Healing Method

W. Bengston, D. Krinsley, "The Effect of the 'Laying On of Hands' on Transplanted Breast Cancer in Mice". *Journal of Scientific Exploration*, Vol. 14(3), pp.353–364, Fall 2000.

W. Bengston, "A Method Used to Train Skeptical Volunteers to Heal in an Experimental Setting". *Journal of Alternative and Complementary Medicine*, vol 13(3), pp. 329–331, 2007.

W. Bengston, M. Moga, "Resonance, Placebo Effects, and Type II Errors: Some Implications from Healing Research for Experimental Methods". *Journal of Alternative and Complementary Medicine*, vol. 13(3), pp. 317–327, May 2007.

W. Bengston, S. Fraser, *"The Energy Cure" – Unraveling the Mystery of Hands-On Healing*. Sounds True, 2010.

M. Moga, W. Bengston, "Anomalous DC Magnetic Field Activity during a Bioenergy Healing Experiment". *Journal of Scientific Exploration*, vol. 24, no. 3, pp. 397–410, 2010.

Background and basics of energy healing. About energy medicine.

P. Aarva, *Parantavat energiat – Myyttistä ja tutkittua tietoa täydentävistä hoidoista*. Viisas Elämä, 2015.

D.J. Benor, *Consciousness, Bioenergy and Healing: Self-Healing and Energy Medicine for the 21st Century*. Wholistic Healing Publications, 2004.

K.S. Cohen, *The Way of Qi Gong: The art and science of Chinese Energy Healing*. New York: Ballantine Books, 1997.

B.M. Dossey, L. Keegan, C.C. Barrere, M.A. Blaszko Helming, *Holistic Nursing – A Handbook for Practice*. Jones & Bartlett Learning, 2016.

D. Eden, *Energy Medicine*. New York: Jeremy P. Tarcher/Putnam. 1998.

C. Eliopoulos, *Invitation to Holistic Health: A Guide to Living a Balanced Life*. Jones & Bartlett Publishers, 2010.

A. Finley-Crosswhite, "Princes and Princely Culture: 1450–1650". *BRILL*. pp. 139–144, 2003.

R. Gerber, *Vibrational Medicine for the 21st Century*. New York: Harper Collins, 2000.

Hayato et al. in J. L. Oschmann's book *Energy Medicine, The Scientific Basis*.

W.L. Hurwitz, "Energy Medicine." In Marc S. Micozzi (editor), *Fundamentals of Complementary and Alternative Medicine* (2nd ed.). Philadelphia, PA: Churchill Livingstone., 2001.

Institute of Noetic Sciences (IONS), *Mapping the Field of Subtle Energy Healing – A web resource for research on energy healing modalities*, http://www.noetic.org/research/projects/mapping-the-field-of-subtle

S. Jain, R. Hammerschlag, P. Mills, L. Cohen, R. Krieger, C. Vieten, S. Lutgendorf, "Clinical Studies of Biofield Therapies: Summary, Methodological Challenges, and Recommendations". *Global Adv*

Health Med, 4, 58–66, 2015, http://www.ncbi.nlm.nih.gov/pmc/articles/
PMC4654788/pdf/gahmj.2015.034.suppl.pdf

E. Kelly, E.W.Kelly ym. *Irreducible mind: Towards a psychology for the
21st century*. Rowman & Littlefied Publishes Inc., 2007.

E. Lane Furdell, *The Royal Doctors, 1485–1714: Medical Personnel at
the Tudor and Stuart Courts*. University Rochester Press, 2001.

Lao-Tzu, *Tao te Ching: A New English Version*. English version and
edition Mitchell S. Harper Collins, 1992.

F. A. Mesmer, *Dissertatio physico-medica de planetarum influxu*
("Physical-medical dissertation on planetary influence"). Vindobonae
(Wien) Ghelen, 1766. https://www.woodlibrarymuseum.org/library/pdf/
ACMZ.pdf

J. L. Oschmann, *Energy Medicine, The Scientific Basis*. London:
Harcourt Publishers, 2000.

M.-M. Stapelberg, *Strange but True – A Historical Background to
Popular Beliefs and Traditions*. Crux Publishing Ltd, 2014.

D.J. Sturdy, *The Royal Touch in England. European Monarchy: Its
Evolution and Practice from Roman Antiquity to Modern Times*. Franz
Steiner Verlag, 1992.

H. Virolainen and I. Virolainen, *Yliluonnollisten Ilmiöiden Ensyklopedia,*
Viisas Elämä, 2014.

Bernard Grad's research studies

B. Grad, R.J. Cadoret ja G.I. Paul, "The influence of an unorthodox method of treatment on wound healing in mice". *International Journal of Parapsychology*,3, 5–24, 1961.

B. Grad, "A Telekinetic Effect on Plant Growth", *International Journal of Parapsychology* Vol. 3, 1961 & Vol 5.,1963.

B. Grad, "A telekinetic effect on plant growth: II. Experiments involving treatment of saline in stoppered bottles", *International Journal of Parapsychology*, Vol. 6, p. 473–478 & p. 484–488, 1964.

B. Grad, "Some Biological Effects of the 'Laying on of Hands': A Review of Experiments with Animals and Plants", *Journal of the American Society for Psychical Research*, Vol. 59, Iss. 2, p. 95–129, 1965.

B. Grad, "The biological effects of "laying on of hands" on animals and plants: Implications for biology",. In book Schmeidler, Gertrude (Toim.), *Parapsychology: Its relation to physics, biology, psychology and psychiatry* (pp. 76–89). Metuchen, NJ: Scarecrow Press, 1976.

Reiki

B. Burden, S. Herron-Marx ja C. Clifford, "The increasing use of Reiki as a complementary therapy in specialist palliative care". *International journal of palliative nursing*, 11(5), 248–253, 2005.

E. Gleisner, "Reiki: The Usui System of Natural Healing". In book P. Coughlin, *Principles and practice of manual therapeutics*. Elsevier Health Sciences. 2002.

L. Johansson, *Reiki – A Key to Your Personal Healing Power*, Lotus Press (WI), 2001.

M.S. Lee, M. H. Pittler ja E. Ernst, "Effects of reiki in clinical practice: a systematic review of randomised clinical trials". *International journal of clinical practice*, 62(6), 947–954, 2008.

S. McGlinn, *Reiki, luonnollisen parantamisen menetelmä*. Gummerus, 2008.

P. Miles, *Reiki: A Comprehensive Guide*. Penguin Books Ltd., 2008.

P. Miles, G. True, "Reiki – Review of a Biofield Therapy: History, Theory, Practice and Research." *Alternative Therapies in Health and Medicine*, 9(2): 62–72, 2003 http://www.reikiinmedicine.org/pdf/alt_therapies_reiki.pdf

The National Center for Complementary and Integrative Health, https://nccih.nih.gov/

N. Pearson, "Foundations of Reiki Ryoho - A Manual of Shoden and Okuden", Healing Arts Press, 2018. https://www.scribd.com/document/365659960/Foundations-of-Reiki-Ryoho

Reiki research: www.centerforreikiresearch.org

R. Schiller, "Reiki: A Starting Point for Integrative Medicine.", *Alternative Therapies in Health and Medicine*. 9(2):20–21, 2003, http://www.reikiinmedicine.org/pdf/schiller.pdf.

A. Vitale, "An integrative review of Reiki touch therapy research." *Holistic Nursing Practice*, 21(4), 167–179, 2007, http://rehab.ucla.edu/workfiles/Urban%20Zen/Integrative_Review_of_Reiki_Research.pdf

Other energy healing methods

D.J. Benor, *Spiritual Healing: Scientific Validation of a Healing Revolution*. Southfield, MI: Vision Publications, 2001.

R. Gordon, *Quantum Touch: The Power of Healing*. Berkley: North Atlantic Books, 1999.

D. Krieger, *Therapeutic Touch as Transpersonal Healing*. Lantern Books. pp. 7–9. 2002.

M.A. Kuhn, *Complementary Therapies for Health Care Providers*, Lippincott Williams & Wilkins, 1999.

R. Van Aken and B. Taylor, "Emerging from depression: The experiential process of Healing Touch explored through grounded theory and case study." *Complementary Therapies in Clinical Practice*, 16, 132–137, 2010.

D.S. Wilkinson, P.L. Knox, J.E. Chatman, T.L. Johnson ym., "The clinical effectiveness of Healing Touch". *The Journal of Alternative and Complementary Medicine*. 8(1), 33–47, 2002.

Energy healing studies

N. Assefi, A. Bogart , J. Goldberg ym., "Reiki for the treatment of fibromyalgia: a randomized controlled trial", *Journal of Alternative and Complementary Medicine*. 14(9):1115–1122, 2008.

J. A. Astin, S. L. Shapiro, D. M. Eisenberg and K. L. Forys, "Mind-body medicine: state of the science, implications for practice", *J. Am. Board. Fam. Pract.* 16(2), 131–147, 2003.

A. L. Baldwin, R. Hammerschlag, "Biofield-based therapies: a systematic review of physiological effects on practitioners during healing" *Explore* (NY).10(3):150-61, May–Jun, 2014.

A. L. Baldwin and G. E. Schwartz, "Personal interaction with a Reiki practitioner decreases noise-induced microvascular damage in an animal model," *Journal of Alternative and Complementary Medicine*, vol. 12, no. 1, pp. 15–22, 2006.

R. Beck, "Mood modification with ELF magnetic fields: A preliminary exploration", Archaeus, 4, 48, 1986. (mainittu J.L. Oscmannin kirjassa *Energy Medicine*)

N. Birocco, C. Guillame, S. Storto, G. Ritorto, C. Catino, N. Gir, L. Balestra, G. Tealdi, C. Orecchia, G.D. Vito, L. Giaretto, M. Donadio, O. Bertetto, M. Schena, L. Ciuffreda, "The effects of Reiki therapy on pain and anxiety in patients attending a day oncology and infusion services unit", *Am J Hosp Palliat Care*. 29(4):290–4, 2012.

D. Bowden, L. Goddard and J. Gruzelier, "A randomised controlled single-blind trial of the effects of Reiki and positive imagery on well-being and salivary cortisol," *Brain Research Bulletin*, vol. 81, no. 1, pp. 66–72, 2010.

G.M. Calaguas, "Survey of college academic stressors: development of a new measure. *Int J Hum Sci*. 9: 441–457, 2012.

D. Bowden, L. Goddard, J. Gruzelier, "A randomised controlled single-blind trial of the efficacy of reiki at benefitting mood and well-being", *Evid Based Complement Alternat Med.* 2011 :381862, 2011.

T. Bunnell, T. "The Effect of "Healing with Intent" on Peak Expiratory Flow Rates in Asthmatics. *Subtle Energies,* 13(1), 2002.

A. Catlin, R.L. Taylor-Ford, "Investigation of standard care versus sham Reiki placebo versus actual Reiki therapy to enhance comfort and well-being in a chemotherapy infusion center", *Oncology Nursing Forum.* 2011;38(3):E212–220.

Dowse and Palmer 1969 in J. L. Oschmann's book *Energy Medicine, The Scientific Basis.*

L. J. Dressen and S. Singg, "Effects of Reiki on pain and selected affective and personality variables of chronically ill patients," *Subtle Energy and Energy Medicine,* vol. 9, pp. 51–82, 1998.

R.S. Friedman, M.M. Burg, P. Miles, F. Lee, R. Lampert, "Effects of reiki on autonomic activity early after acute coronary syndrome." *J Am Coll Cardiol.* 2010 Sep 14;56(12):995-6. http://reikiinmedicine.org/pdf/jacc.pdf

S. N. Garland, D. Valentine, K. Desai ym., "Complementary and alternative medicine use and benefit finding among cancer patients," *Journal of Alternative and Complementary Medicine,* vol. 19, no. 11, pp. 876–881, 2013.

M. George, and M. Topaz, "A systematic review of complementary and alternative medicine for asthma self-management", *Nursing Clinics of North America,* 48(1), 53–149, 2013.

G. Gronowicz, E. R. Secor Jr, J. R. Flynn, E. R. Jellison, L. T. Kuhn, "Therapeutic Touch Has Significant Effects on Mouse Breast Cancer Metastasis and Immune Responses but Not Primary Tumor Size", *Evid Based Complement Alternat Med.* 2015: 926565, 2015.

T. Hisamitsu, A. Seto, S. Nakazato, T. Yamamoto and S. K. Aung, "Emission of extremely strong magnetic fields from the head and whole body during oriental breathing exercises." *Acupuncture & Electrotherapeutics Research*, 21(3–4), 219–227, 1996

G. S. Hubbard, E. C. May and H. E. Puthoff, "Possible production of photons during a remote viewing task: Preliminary results", *Research in Parapsychology* 1985, toim. D. H. Weiner and D. I. Radin. Metuchen, NJ: Scarecrow Press, 1986.

A. Kundu, Y. Lin, A.P. Oron et al. "Reiki therapy for postoperative oral pain in pediatric patients: pilot data from a double-blind, randomized clinical trial", *Complementary Therapies in Clinical Practice.* 2014;20(1):21–25.

M. S. Lee, "Is reiki beneficial for pain management?. *Focus on Alternative and Complementary Therapies*, 13(2), 78–81, 2008.

M. S. Lee, M. H. Pittler, E. Ernst, "Effects of Reiki in clinical practice: a systematic review of randomised clinical trials", *International Journal of Clinical Practice.* 62(6):947–954, 2008.

N. Mackay, S. Hansen and O. McFarlane, "Autonomic nervous system changes during Reiki treatment: a preliminary study", *Journal of Alternative and Complementary Medicine*, 10(6):1077–81. May 2004.

N. Mackay, S. Hansen, and O. McFarlane, "Autonomic nervous system changes during Reiki treatment: a preliminary study," *Journal of Alternative and Complementary Medicine*, vol. 10, no. 6, pp. 1077–1081, 2004.

A. A. Mansour, M. Beuche, G. Laing, A. Leis, J. Nurse, " A study to test the effectiveness of placebo Reiki standardization procedures developed for a planned Reiki efficacy study", *J Altern Complement Med*. 5(2):153–164, 1999.

P. Miles, "Reiki for Support of Cancer Patients". *Advances in Mind-Body Medicine*. Fall 22(2):20-26, 2007. http://advancesjournal.com/ pdfarticles/miles.pdf

L. Nield-Anderson, A. Ameling, "Reiki: a complementary therapy for nursing practice.", *Journal of Psychosocial Nursing and Mental Health Services*. 39(4):42–49, 2001.

Ogawa et al. In D. J. Benor's book *Spiritual Healing: Scientific Validation of a Healing Revolution*.

J.L. Oschman, *Energy Medicine in Therapeutics and Human Performance*. Elsevier, 2003.

K. Olson, J. Hanson, "Using Reiki to manage pain: a preliminary report", *Cancer Prev Control.*, 1(2):108-113, 1997.

R.R. Pavek, *Handbook of SHEN*. Sausalito, CA: SHEN Therapy Institute, 1987.

H. E. Puthoff, "Information transmission under conditions of sensory shielding". *Nature*, 251(18), 602–607, 1974.

D. Radin, M. Schlitz, C. Baur, Distant Healing Intention Therapies: An Overview of the Scientific Evidence, *Glob Adv Health Med.* 2015 Nov; 4, 67, http://www.ncbi.nlm.nih.gov/pmc/articles/PMC4654780/

S. Schmidt, R. Schneider, J. Utts and H. Walach, "Distant intentionality and the feeling of being stared at: Two meta-analyses", *British Journal of Psychology*, 95, 235-247, 2004.

G.E. Schwartz, W.L. Simon, *The Energy Healing Experiments: Science Reveals Our Natural Power To Heal.* New York, NY: Atria Books, 2007.

A. Seto, C. Kusaka, S. Nakazato, W. Huang, T. Sato et al., "Detection of extraordinary large bio-magnetic field strength from human hand during external qi emission", *Acupuncture & Electro-therapeutics Research*, 17, 75–94, 1992.

A. G. Shore, "Long-term effects of energetic healing on symptoms of psychological depression and self-perceived stress", *Alternative Therapies in Health and Medicine*, vol. 10, no. 3, pp. 42–48, 2004.

L. Sidorov, "The imprinting and transmission of mentally-directed bioinformation", 2002. http:// www.emergentmind.org/ original_articles.htm

S. Thrane, S. M. Cohen, "Effect of Reiki therapy on pain and anxiety in adults: an in-depth literature review of randomized trials with effect size calculations.", *Pain Management Nursing.* February 27, 2014.

S. VanderVaart, V. M. Gijsen, S. N. de Wildt et al., "A systematic review of the therapeutic effects of Reiki", *Journal of Alternative and Complementary Medicine.* 15(11):1157–1169, 2009.

D. W. Wardell and J. Engebretson, "Biological correlates of reiki touch healing," *Journal of Advanced Nursing*, vol. 33, no. 4, pp. 439–445, 2001.

W. Wetzel, "Reiki Healing: a physiologic perspective," *Journal of Holistic Nursing*, vol. 7, no. 1, pp. 47–154, 1989.

Wever 1969 J. L. Oschmann's book *Energy Medicine, The Scientific Basis*.

D. P. Wirth, D. R. Brenlan, R. J. Levine, and C. M. Rodriguez, "The effect of complementary healing therapy on postoperative pain after surgical removal of impacted third molar teeth," *Complementary Therapies in Medicine*, vol. 1, no. 3, pp. 133–138, 1993.

D. P. Wirth, R. J. Chang, W. S. Eidelman, and J. B. Paxton, "Haematological indicators of complementary healing intervention," *Complementary Therapies in Medicine*, vol. 4, no. 1, pp. 14–20, 1996.

R. Wiseman and M. Schlitz,. "Experimenter effects and the remote detection of staring", *The Journal of Parapsychology*, Vol. 61, September 1997.

J. Zimmerman, "Laying-on-of-hands healing and therapeutic touch: a testable theory. BEMI Currents, *Journal of the BioElectroMagnetics Institute*, 2, 8–17, 1990.

Articles related to different senses and emotions

R. Chillot, *Psychology Today*, The Power of Touch, https://www.psychologytoday.com/articles/201302/the-power-touch

S. Hayano, "Measuring Qi Energy", 2006, http://www.equilibrium-e3.com/images/PDF/Measuring%20Qi%20Energy.pdf

R. McCraty, M., Atkinson, W.A. Tiller and G Rein, "New Electrophysiological Correlates Associated With Intentional Heart Focus". *Subtle Energies*, 4 (3):251-262, 1995.

L. Nummenmaa, E. Glereana, R. Hari and J. K. Hietanen, "Bodily maps of emotions" *PNAS*, vol. 111 (2), 646–651, 2013. http://www.pnas.org/content/111/2/646.full

D.H. Powell, http://dianehennacypowell.com/consciousness/telepathy-project/

HearthMath Institute, "Science of the Heart – Exploring the Role of the Heart in Human Performance. An Overview of Research Conducted by the HeartMath Institute." https://www.heartmath.org/resources/downloads/science-of-the-heart/

E. Seppälä, *The Happiness Track, How to Apply the Science of Happiness to Accelerate Your Success*. Harper Collin Publishers, 2016.

Growth speed of plants

B. Grad's articles: see above under topic: Research Studies of Bernard Grad's

R. Miller, "The Positive Effect of Prayer on Plants," Psychic, April 1972. (in L. McTaggart's book *The Intention Experiment,* Free Press, 2007).

Spindrift group is mentioned in W. L. Rand's book *Reiki for a New Millennium*, B. Jain Publishers, Ltd., 2000.

Philosophy and mind & consciousness

R. G. Andhn and B. J. Dunne, "The PEAR Proposition", *Journal of Scientific Exploration*, Vol. 19, No. 2, pp. 195–245, 2005. http://www.princeton.edu/~pear/pdfs/2005-pear-proposition.pdf

H. Atmanspacher, "Quantum Approaches to Consciousness", *The Stanford Encyclopedia of Philosophy*. Ed. Edward N. Zalta, 2015. http://plato.stanford.edu/archives/sum2015/entries/qt-consciousness/

J. Belt, A. Ovaska, P. Telakivi, "Millaista on olla tietoinen? – David Chalmersin helpot ja vaikeat kysymykset", *niin & näin* 3/15, 2015, http://netn.fi/artikkeli/millaista-on-olla-tietoinen-david-chalmersin-helpot-ja-vaikeat-kysymykset

D. Bohm, "A new theory of the relationship of mind and matter". *Philosophical Psychology*, 3(2): 271–286, 1990.

D. Bohm, and B. Hiley, *The undivided universe: An ontological interpretation of quantum theory*. Routledge, NY, 1993.

O. Burkeman, "Why can't the world's greatest minds solve the mystery of consciousness?", *The Guardian*, 21.1.2015.

D.J. Chalmers, *The Conscious Mind. In Search for a Fundamental Theory*. Oxford University Press, New York 1996.

D. Chalmers and David Bourget, Online Papers on Consciousness, Australian National University. http://consc.net/online, 7000+ julkaisua tietoisuudesta.

D. Radin, M. Emoto, T. Kizu, N. Lund, "Effects of Distant Intention on Water Crystal Formation: A Triple-Blind Replication", http://www.noetic.org/research/projects/effects-of-distant-intention-on

M. Emoto, *The Hidden Messages in Water*, Beyond Words Publishing, Inc., Oregon, 2004.

W. Buckingham, D. Burnham, C. Hill, P.J. King, J. Marenbon, M. Weeks ym. The Philosophy Book, DK, 2001, (Finnish edition: J. Korhonen and S. Korpela, *Filosofit*, Schildts & Söderströms, 2011).

The Global Consciousness Project: Meaningful Correlations in Random Data, http://noosphere.princeton.edu/

R. C. Henry, "The Mental Universe"; *Nature* 436:29, 2005.

B. J. Hiley and P. Pylkkanen, "Can Mind Affect Matter Via Active Information?", *Mind & Matter,* Vol. 3(2), 7, 2005.

T. Kallio-Tamminen, *Kvanttilainen todellisuus – fysiikka ja filosofia maailmankuvan muovaajina.* Gaudeamus, Helsinki 2008.

E. F. Kelly, A. Crabtree ja P. Marshall, *Beyond Physicalism: Toward Reconciliation of Science and Spirituality.* Rowman & Littlefield, 2015.

K. V. Laurikainen, *Filosofiaa fyysikon silmin.* Yliopistopaino, Helsinki, 1991.

T. Nagel, *Mind and Cosmos: Why the Materialist Neo-Darwinian Conception of Nature Is Almost Certainly False,* Oxford University Press, 2012. *(suom. L. Snellman, Mieli and kosmos, Miksi materialis-darwinistinen luontokäsitys on lähes varmasti epätosi, Basam Books, 2014).*

A. Pais, *The Genius of Science*. Oxford, Oxford University Press, 2000, 210-262.

P. Pylkkänen, "Kvanttiteoria filosofian innoittajana", *niin & näin* 3/15, 2015. http://netn.fi/artikkeli/kvanttiteoria-filosofian-innoittajana

P. Pylkkänen, *Mind, Matter and Implicate Order*. Springer Verlag 2007.

D. Radin, *Entangled Minds: Extrasensory Experiences in a Quantum Reality*. New York, NY: Paraview Pocket Books, 2006.

D. Radin, D. Ferrari, "Effects of consciousness on the fall of dice: a metaanalysis", *J. Scientific Exploration* 1991, 5, 61–8376.

D. Radin, L. Michel, K. Galdamez, P. Wendland, R. Rickenbach and Arnaud Delorme, "Consciousness and the double-slit interference pattern: Six experiments", *Physics Essays 2012,* 25, 2, http://www.deanradin.com/evidence/Radin2012doubleslit.pdf

D. Radin, G. Hayssen, M Emoto and T. Kizu, "Double-blind test of the effects of distant intention on water crystal formation", *Explore*, 2:408–411, 2006.

R. Sheldrake, *"Science Delusion",*Coronet, 2012.

N. Tesla, *My Inventions: The Autobiography of Nikola Tesla*, Electrical Experimenter, 1919.

J. Verne, *Journey to the Centre of the Earth,* Bantam, 2006 (first published 1864) (suomentanut Pentti Kähkönen, *Matka maan keskipisteeseen.* WSOY, 1974).

Mind and healing

D.J. Benor, "Survey of Spiritual Healing Research", *Complementary Medical Research*, 4:9–33, 1990.

L. Dossey, *Healing Words: The Power of Prayer and the Practice of Medicine.* New York: Harper San Francisco 1993.

A. J. Espay, M. M. Norris, J. C. Eliassen, A. Dwivedi, M. S. Smith, C. Banks, J. B. Allendorfer, A. E. Lang, D. E. Fleck, M. J. Linke, and J. P. Szaflarski, Placebo effect of medication cost in Parkinson disease, A randomized double-blind study, *Neurology*, January 28, 2015, http://www.neurology.org/content/early/2015/01/28/WNL.0000000000001282

T. Kaptchuk ym., Placebos without deception: A randomized controlled trial in irritable bowel syndrome. *PLoS ONE*, 2010, http://media.virbcdn.com/files/a4/FileItem-112336-KaptchukPLoSOne2010.pdf (see also: http://harvardmagazine.com/2013/01/the-placebo-phenomenon).

K. Krieger, Healing by the "Laying-on" of hands as a facilitator of bioenergetic change: The response of in-vivo human hemoglobin, *Psychoenergetic Systems*, Vol. 1, p. 121–129, 1976.

L. McTaggart, *The Intention Experiment: Using Your Thoughts to Change Your Life and the World,* Free Press, 2007.

D. Radin and E. Lobach, "Toward Understanding the Placebo Effect: Investigating a Possible Retrocausal Factor", *Journal of Alternative and Complementary Medicine*, Vol. 13(7), 733, 2007, http://www.deanradin.com/evidence/Radin2007RetroCausal.pdf.

L. Rankin, *Mind over Medicine: Scientific Proof You Can Heal Yourself,* Hay House, Inc., 2013.

H. Virolainen & I. Virolainen, *Mielen voima – Mielen vaikutus terveyteen ja hyvinvointiin,* Viisas Elämä, 2016.

S.S. Wang, "Why Placebos Work Wonders," *Wall Street Journal,* January 10, 2012, http://online.wsj.com/article/SB10001424052970204720204577128873886471982.html.

About fields

A. L. Baldwin, W. L. Rand and G. E. Schwartz, "Practicing Reiki Does Not Appear to Routinely Produce High-Intensity Electromagnetic Fields from the Heart or Hands of Reiki Practitioners, *The Journal of Alternative and Complementary Medicine,* Vol. 0, Number 0, 2013, pp. 1–9. http://www.ncbi.nlm.nih.gov/pubmed/23210468

R. O. Becker, "Exploring New Horizons in Electromedicine.", *J Alt Comp Med,* 10(4), 2004. Becker also in J. L. Oschmann's book *Energy Medicine, The Scientific Basis.*

D. E. McCarty, S. Carrubba, A. L. Chesson, C. Frilot, E. Gonzalez-Toledo, A. A. Marino, "Electromagnetic Hypersensitivity: Evidence for a Novel Neurological Syndrome". *Int. J. Neurosci.* 121(12):670-6, 2011. http://www.ncbi.nlm.nih.gov/pubmed/21793784

R. McCraty, M. Atkinson, W. A. Tiller and G. Rein, "New Electrophysiological Correlates Associated With Intentional Heart Focus". *Subtle Energies,* 4 (3):251–262, 1995.

S.L. Fahrion, M. Wirkus and P. Pooley, "EEG Amplitude, Brain Mapping and Synchrony in and Between a Bioenergy Practitioner and Client During Healing", *Subtle Energies Journal*, Vol. 1, No. 3, 1992.

Einthoven in J.L. Oschmann's book *Energy Medicine, The Scientific Basis*.

L. McTaggart, *The Field: The Quest for the Secret Force of the Universe*, Free Press, 2003.

PEMF (Pulsed Electromagnetic Field Therapy) in J. L. Oschmann's book *Energy Medicine, The Scientific Basis*.

K. Schlegel and M. Füllekrug, "50 Years of Schumann Resonance", published originally in *Physik in unserer Zeit*, 33(6), 256–26, 2002. https://www.scribd.com/doc/228596266/50-Years-of-Schumann-Resonance

G. E. Schwartz, S. Swanick, W. Sibert, D. A. Lewis, S. E. Lewis, L. Nelson, I. R. Bell, "Biofield detection: role of bioenergy awareness training and individual differences in absorption". *Journal of Alternative & Complementary Medicine*, 10 (1), 167–169, 2004.

Science of the Heart: Exploring the Role of the Heart in Human Performance. HeartMath Research Center, the Institute of HeartMath.

M. Wyde, M. Cesta, C. Blystone, S. Elmore, P. Foster, M. Hooth, G. Kissling, D. Malarkey, R. Sills, M. Stout, N. Walker, K. Witt, M. Wolfe, J. Bucher, "Report of Partial findings from the National Toxicology Program Carcinogenesis Studies of Cell Phone Radiofrequency Radiation in Hsd: Sprague Dawley® SD rats (Whole Body Exposure)", *bioRxiv* 055699, http://biorxiv.org/content/early/2016/05/26/055699

About energy and quantum physics

D. Bodanis, $E=mc^2$ – A Biography of the World's Most Famous Equation, Berkley Publishing Group, 2001. (suom. Ilkka Rekiaro, $E=mc^2$ – Maailman tunnetuimman yhtälön elämäkerta, Tammi, 2000).

R. Feynman, "The Distinction of Past and Future, from The Character of Physical Law", 1965, http://www.feynmanlectures.caltech.edu/

J. Hagelin, "Dr. John Hagelin: Veda and Physics: The Science and Technology of the Unified Field", https://www.youtube.com/watch?v=4u3f7_p1i8c

W. Moore, *A Life of Erwin Schrodinger*. Cambridge University Press, Canto reprint, 1994.

B. Rosenblum and Fred Kuttner, *Quantum Enigma*, Oxford University Press, 2006.

E. Schrödinger, *What is Life?* Cambridge Press, 1967. http://web.mit.edu/philosophy/religionandscience/mindandmatter.pdf

B. Sommers, *Erwin Schrödinger and Vedic Philosophy* http://www.scribd.com/doc/173472359/Erwin-Schrodinger-and-Vedic-Philosophy#scribd

H. Stapp, *Mind, Matter and Quantum Mechanics*. Springer, New York 1993.

Entanglement

J. Bub, "Quantum Entanglement and Information", *The Stanford Encyclopedia of Philosophy*. Toim. Edward N. Zalta. 2015. http://plato.stanford.edu/archives/sum2015/entries/qt-entangle/

P. G. Kwiat, S. Barraza-Lopez, A. Stefanov, N. Gisin, "Experimental entanglement distillation and 'hidden' non-locality", *Nature*, 409(6823): 1014–7, 2001.

D. Radin, *Entangled minds*. New York: Simon & Schuster; 2006

Science: 75 years of Entanglement, Vol. 178 (11), November 20, p. 25, 2010. https://www.sciencenews.org/article/75-years-entanglement

Distant healing

Distant healing studies and articles: http://noetic.org/research/projects/compassionate-intention-prayer-and-distant-healing/reading

L. Dossey, "How Healing Happens: Exploring the Nonlocal Gap", *Alternative Therapies in Health and Medicine* 8(2)12–16, 103–110, 2002, http://www.noetic.org/sites/default/files/uploads/files/HowHealingHappens.pdf

Institute of Noetic Sciences: Selected Peer-Reviewed Journal Publications on Psi Research, http://www.noetic.org/research/psi-research

D. Radin, M. Schlitz, C. Baur, "Distant Healing Intention Therapies: An Overview of the Scientific Evidence", *Glob Adv Health Med.* 4(Suppl): 67–71, Nov. 2015, http://www.ncbi.nlm.nih.gov/pmc/articles/PMC4654780/

D. Radin, "Selected Psi Research Publications", http://deanradin.com/evidence/evidence.htm

Inner wisdom

A. Einstein, *On Cosmic Religion and Other Opinions and Aphorisms*, Covici-Friede, Inc., 1931.

H. Poincaré, translated to engl. F. Maitland, *Science and Method*, T. Nelson, 1914.

A. Webb, "6 Times Dreams and Mysticism Changed the Course of Science", http://ultraculture.org/blog/2016/03/30/dreams-intuition-science/

Appendix 1. Sample self-healing positions

1. Turning inward: First, put both hands over your eyes.
2. Calming down: Put both hands on the top of your head (the crown chakra).
3. Intuition: Put the other hand on the back of your head and the other hand on the forehead (the third eye).
4. Listening: Put the hands on both sides of the head over the ears and the jaw joints.
5. Expression: Put one hand on the neck and the other on the throat (the throat chakra). If it feels better, you can just put both hands on the throat.
6. Heart: Put the hands to the chest on top (the heart chakra) or next to each other.
7. The ribs: Put the palms of your hands on both sides over the ribs (solar plexus).
8. The abdomen: Put both hands next to each other on the abdomen (sacral chakra).
9. The groin: Put one hand on the left and the other on the right groin (root chakra).
10. The knees: Take hold of one knee from the front with one hand and from underneath with the other hand. First treat one knee and then the other one.
11. The feet: Put one hand under the sole of one foot, and the other hand, from the opposite side, over the foot. Then treat the other foot.
12. The buttocks: Sit on your hands, with the palms to the buttocks.

13. Lower back: Put your palms against the lower back (easiest with the fingers pointing downward).
14. The upper back and shoulders: Treat both sides at the same time: put your left palm on the left shoulder and the right palm on the right shoulder.

Appendix 2. Onion-peeling exercise

In the exercise, you undo roles that you have adopted, gathered and built for yourself. When doing the exercise the first few times, you can list some of your roles before getting started, such as mother or father, daughter or son, spouse, master, doctor, director, and so on. Then, in the exercise you will imagine these one at a time.

If you like, you can ask someone else to read out the exercise, and close your eyes for the duration of the exercise.

1. Take a deep breath in – and a deep breath out.
2. Breathe in a feeling of relaxation and well-being – and breathe out all the tensions and bad feelings.
3. Feel, how, with each breath out, you let go a little more. Let go of all the thoughts that go through your head – if any of them is of essential importance, it will come back to your mind when needed.
4. Every breath out will help you let go a little more.
5. Then, move your attention from the breath to yourself. Imagine yourself in miniature size and look at yourself from the outside.
6. Gradually start unraveling roles around you – just as if you were peeling an onion. You can go over the roles that you have listed beforehand, or you can observe the roles that pop into your mind when you think of yourself and some of your essential roles.

7. Pay attention to each role, one at a time, and think about what it gives to you. What is good, and what is bad about it? Each time, after having processed a role in your mind, let go of it.

8. As you are dropping a role, pay attention to the feelings that the role evokes in you. Does releasing it create physical sensations, too?

9. Who is gradually revealed from underneath the roles, and what it is that remains?

Appendix 3. Working through your emotions exercise

Ask someone else to read the exercise to you. Close your eyes during the exercise.

1. Take a few deep breaths in, and out.
2. Imagine in your mind, how a small, white pearl is dropped inside of you, as if fell into a pond. The pearl floats inside you as if in a small pond.
3. The pearl floats, drifts everywhere, and goes to every corner of your body. It moves at its own pace.
4. In your mind, you can also carry the pearl and feel how it moves faster at times, and slower at others.
5. At times it may feel like the pearl gets stuck; it can linger for a little longer in some places.
6. Now you can let the pearl go where it wants to stop the most. Give the pearl a little time. If you have difficulties finding a place where the pearl would most like to stop, you can try stopping it in one place and then move it to another one. Does the new place feel better than the old one? You still can try moving the pearl to another place, and do it again, if this feels like an easier way to find the best place to stop.
7. When you have found a good spot, you can stay there and listen to the feelings that come up the strongest. Which is the strongest feeling?
8. Follow the feeling. Are you able to recognize what causes it? What is it that turns up the strongest? What thoughts arise?

9. If you want, you can also contemplate what is the opposite of the feeling that you have. What do you really want?
10. Visualize the Reiki Sei Hei Ki –symbol and let it work.
11. Let go of everything, of all thoughts, and just be present. You are enough just the way you are.

Appendix 4. Heart-mind meditation

If you want, you can ask someone else to read the meditation to you. In that case, close your eyes for the duration of the meditation.

1. Bring your attention to your breath. Breathe in and out... When you breathe in, say "I let", and when you breathe out, say "go". "I let... go..." In and out...
2. Continue, keeping your attention on the breath, and at the same time, let go of everything that is on your mind: of all the thoughts, all the hopes, absolutely everything. Keep doing this for a little while and let the mind be emptied.
3. Then bring the attention to your own heart. Take a moment to listen and see how you are feeling. How do you feel right now? What do you feel? Which feeling or issue surfaces to the top? Try to see underneath the feeling. What is underneath it? Are you able to recognize what causes the feeling? Not everything will be opened up at once; the recognizing can take repeated practice. If you want, you can return to the exercise later. It is possible for the processing to continue in your dreams during the following nights.
4. Focus on listening to your heart for some time. Feel eventually, how love fills your whole heart. Let it really fill it. Feel the pureness, the clarity, the light, and the love.
5. The feeling of love, pureness, clarity and light filling your mind and spreading around you, and from there on, everywhere.
6. Gradually come back, feeling refreshed, radiating with love and positivity.

Appendix 5. Increasing your flow of qi

Ball of energy

The ball of energy exercise is one of the most common exercises used in different energy healing methods, and it can be used to observe the flow of *qi*.

1. Hold your hands so that the palms are facing each other at about a few inches distance.
2. Close your eyes and breathe deeply.
3. Bring your attention to the space in between the hands.
4. Move the hands further out, to about two feet from each other.
5. Bring them close to each other again, so that they almost touch each other.
6. Repeat the steps 4 and 5 slowly and gently for two minutes. Pay attention all the time to the feeling between your hands. Try rubbing the hands against each other, if, after a couple of minutes you still cannot feel anything in your hands.
7. Move the hands again to two feet's distance, and move them slowly toward each other. At some point, you will start feeling resistance, as if magnets were repelling each other.
8. Now, imagine that the energy is a ball, and rotate it between your hands.
9. You can also try growing the size of the ball or squeeze the ball together to shrink it, and see how it feels.

Increasing the flow of qi in the palms 1

1. Feel the tips of your fingers: hold one hand in the air with the fingers apart, and bring your attention to the feeling in the fingertips.
2. Pay attention to the feeling in the fingertips for a couple of minutes. You may feel tingling in the fingertips, stinging, vibrating, or a sense of heat or weight. If you don't feel anything, still keep your attention on the fingertips and imagine how someone is just reaching to give you an object.

Increasing the flow of qi in the palms 2 (an exercise in pairs)

1. Ask your partner to hold their left hand in front of them with the palm facing up.
2. Put your right hand a couple of inches above your partner's palm, with the palm facing down toward theirs.
3. Change distance, and seek for the distance where you can "feel" your partner's palm the best.
4. Ask your partner to hold their hand in place, and move your palm slowly, with small rotating movements, anticlockwise around the center of the palm (with the palm kept open and facing downward all the time), as if you were turning a screw into your partner's palm.
5. Gradually increase the size of the circle that you are making and think that your palm is radiating light toward your partner's palm and fingertips, and also to the wrists.
6. Having rotated for a while, change direction and rotate clockwise.
7. Ask your partner to describe what they felt. What did rotating the palm anticlockwise feel like? And how about clockwise?

Increasing the flow of qi in the body (an exercise in pairs)

There are two ways to do the exercise, either by grounding, that is by seeking a connection to the ground, in which case one starts from the feet, or by seeking a connection to the source of *qi* through the crown chakra, in which case one starts from the head.

1. Lie on the floor with your back on a mat.
2. Ask your partner to brush lightly with their fingertips starting from the soles of your feet and moving toward the ankles (or from the top of your head toward your forehead), and then to take a break.
3. Focus on the feeling of the touching, and try to hold the feeling in your mind for as long as possible.
4. When you are ready, ask your partner to continue by brushing again from where they left off. Again, hold on to the feeling for as long as possible in your mind.
5. Continue in the same way, this time all the way to the head (or to the feet, if you started from the top of the head), and from there, to the hands.
6. Repeat the exercise with longer strokes. If you have difficulty feeling a certain spot, ask your partner to repeat the stroke again over the same spot. If, after your partner's stroke, you still don't feel anything, move on.
7. Repeat the exercise with one whole-body stroke.
   a. If you started from the feet, ask you partner to do the stroking from the feet up toward the head, and from head to the hands, and all the way to the fingertips.

289

b. If you started from the top of the head, ask your partner to do the stroking from the top of the head to the feet, and back again to the shoulders, and over the arms to the hands, all the way to the fingertips.

8. After the exercise, try to bring back to mind the entire experience and how it felt in your body. Repeat the exercise until it is easy for you to bring back the sensation in the whole body all at once.

9. Then, repeat the stroking over the body on the backside, either from the feet toward the top of the head, or from the top of the head to the feet.

10. After this, try to bring back to mind the feeling of stroking over the whole body. You can practice the feeling of increasing the energy in your mind whenever you want. You can also include the breath in the exercise, breathing the energy in from the feet to the top of the head (or the other way around), or breathing the energy out to the arms, and all the way to the fingertips.

The qigong tree-exercise

1. Ground the feet firmly to the ground. First, lift the toes up and then bring them firmly down to the ground one at a time.
2. Lift your hands up as the branches of a tree.
3. Close your eyes.
4. Hold your attention on the branches (your hands), and observe the feeling. Imagine, how the wind blows through the branches, although you are standing firmly on the ground. Nothing can shake you: you are in balance, grounded both physically and mentally.
5. Finally, listen to how you feel and return to this moment.

About the author

Johanna Blomqvist, Ph.D. is a physicist, author, speaker, Reiki master teacher, energy healer and hypnosis practitioner.

She is on a mission to combine science and spirituality and help people move "beyond materialism". She encourages everyone to challenge their worldview whether it is by energy healing method or something else.

You can find more about Johanna's work from www.johannablomqvist.com

Back cover material

What is the "energy" transmitted in energy healing?
What can science and research say about energy healing?
Doesn't modern science rule out phenomena like this?
Does energy healing work and, if so, how?

Physicist Johanna Blomqvist's book will give answers to these questions.

Astonishing accounts of healings omitted by mainstream media led her to a journey that is still continuing. In the book, she tells about her path to energy healing and her own extraordinary experiences. The obvious question was how to fit these experiences to the scientific model she had learned.

Energy healing and such topics as subtle energy, the effect of mind on healing and remote healing are usually perplexing to those used to an everyday materialistic worldview. In the book, energy healing is approached from the viewpoint of known modern science. Could quantum physics give answers to energy healing? After all, one could say that according to quantum physics, we are all one and the same vibrating energy at the subatomic level. Besides quantum physics, the book also addresses the questions of mind and consciousness.

The book has been written as an aid to those who wish to broaden their horizons or are already practicing energy healing, yet could use tools for telling others about it. The book is also meant for everyone who may be seeking support from complementary medicine.

Made in the USA
Las Vegas, NV
19 December 2021